Dee: Be en
(

How to
Get Over Yourself, Get Out of Your Own Way, and Get What YOU Want Out of Life!

In 7 Life-Changing Steps

Beatrice Bruno

Unattributed quotations are by Beatrice Bruno

Unless otherwise indicated, Scripture quotations are from the King James Version of the Holy Bible.

Published by Heard Word Publishing, LLC
1980 Van Buren Way
Aurora, CO 80011

How to Get Over Yourself, Get Out of Your Own Way, and Get What YOU Want Out of Life!

ISBN-13: 978-0-9801060-3-9

Copies of *How To Get Over Yourself, Get Out of Your Own Way,, and Get What YOU Want Out of Life!* are available at www.TheGetOverItGal.com.

DEDICATION

This book is dedicated to the M.O.O.D. Squad (Move Over Or Dance!) Susan and Helen from Denver, Colorado; honorary member Angela from Queens, New York; honorary member Carolyn from Clarksville, Tennessee.

If you are interested in becoming an honorary M.O.O.D. Squad member, please write to me at Beatrice@TheGetOverItGal.com.

Each of us is in the process of Getting Over Ourselves. We are not afraid to learn something new (and scary) about ourselves in the process.

Thanks, Ladies, for being you: FOR REAL!

CONTENTS

ACKNOWLEDGMENTS

Thine, O Lord, is the greatness, and the power, and the glory, and the victory, and the majesty: for all that is in the heaven and in the earth is Thine; Thine is the kingdom, O Lord, and Thou art exalted as head above all. *I Chronicles 29:11*

Thank You, Lord, for Your mercy and grace in my life! You have kept me through this process of Getting Over Myself; You never left me. Thank You for Your patience as I messed up over and over again and discouraged myself to the point that I didn't want to go any further. Lord, You are so precious to me! I love You!

To my husband, my Boo, John P. Bruno, Sr.: you are the most patient man alive! I love you and thank God for you each and every day!

To my children: Tara, William, John Jr., EJ, and niece, Jakeia: I love you! Get Over Yourselves (never heard *that* before; riiight!) The best is yet to come!

To Joe Sabah and Diana Hall: God bless you for mentoring and believing in me.

DISCLAIMER:

To all Soldiers in the Army of Life:

ATTENTION!!!!

The Drill Sergeant Is IN!

For the next nine (9) chapters, you will receive instruction in:

- Getting Over Yourself
- Getting Out of Your Own Way
- Getting What You Want Out of Life

I have personally trained long and hard to ***get over myself, get out of my own way, and to get what I want in life***.

It has been a rough road but well worth all I have been through! I do not despise my training! Although not always enjoyable, it has been informative. My training has given me the authority I need to instruct YOU!

Uncle Sam needed me for the US Army! The World at Large needs YOU to be all YOU can be, do all YOU can do, and have all YOU can have!

It is your turn! It is your season!

I will be your Drill Sergeant for as long as it takes to get you to where you NEED to be. I will not mollycoddle or enable you. I will be

IN YOUR FACE!

THIS IS NOT A TEST!

LIFE IS REAL!

LIFE IS HARD!

YOU want something different in your life. I am here to help you get what you want! Almighty God, your Creator, depends on you to give it ALL you've got! Your family depends on you! Others depend on you! YOU depend on YOU!

By purchasing this book, you have signed up for the first three phases of *Get Over Yourself Boot-Camp*! The training is fierce; it is not for the weak of heart!

This book may not be for you!

Introduction

As an active duty soldier in the US Army, my greatest achievement and delight was serving as a Basic Combat Training Drill Sergeant at Fort Dix, New Jersey. They were the best of times for me; they were the worst of times for my soldiers!

I underwent nine weeks of training to turn new recruits into soldiers. That one extra week of training helped me be effective in my assignment as a Drill Sergeant. It worked!

Over an eight-week period, couch potatoes masquerading as Privates were turned into lean, mean, fighting machines. What a job!

We succeeded! The vast majority of the almost 2000 soldiers I assisted in training over a two-year period are some of the same soldiers you see today traveling through our airports as they return from various war hotspots our military forces occupy.

It was my honor and privilege to have had a hand in their initial training in the US Army.

Once I left the military, I returned to the Army of Life. I had forgotten about *this* Army. I had forgotten that every human being serves in this Army; whether they want to or not. It was completely different from what I had become accustomed to for nearly two decades.

I no longer knew what was expected of me in the Army of Life. I had forgotten the so-called pecking order of things. Unfortunately, I soon remembered.

As I got back in the groove of things, I found it very comfortable to help as many people as I could get to where they wanted to go. But, there was no reciprocation. As a matter of fact, the more I gave, the more was taken from me.

I more or less lost my identity as I became a Bridesmaid Extraordinaire! I was the "Yes" girl to anyone who needed it. I forgot about being a soldier; I forgot how to be myself.

I forgot that soldiers always stood on their post and accomplished their mission; regardless of the circumstances or situation they encountered.

I forget that, as a soldier, I was a leader; I was to lead by example. Instead of leading by example, I became everyone else's follower.

Now, I'm not saying there is anything wrong with helping others; but, you have a job to do as well! At some point in life, you forgot how to soldier. You allowed life and other forces to overpower you causing you to **get in your own way!**

NO MORE! GET OVER YOURSELF!

Using all I have learned over three decades, I will help you gain better footing of your place in the Army of Life.

THIS BOOK IS FOR YOU!

How to Get Over Yourself, Get Out of Your Own Way, and Get What You Want Out of Life! is centered on folks suffering from what I call the "Bridesmaid Syndrome." This is not a for-women-only syndrome; men suffer from it as well (Bridesmaid Syndrome is a little more catchy than Groomsman Syndrome!)

These precious people find themselves **always** being the Bridesmaid or Groomsman and **never** the Bride or Groom.

I must give you fair warning: I am going to cause you to look at yourself as never before. Unless you have lived the life of a Saint, you will not like what you see! Little story first:

I recently spent 13.5 months in New York taking care of my Dad; he had to have a couple eye surgeries. While there, thousands of miles away from family and friends in Colorado, I spent much time praying, fasting, and meditating on the Word of God (which I love.)

What I didn't love were the things I saw about myself during all this time I had on my hands. Pure ugliness!

I discovered that I had completely left off the purpose I was created for. I discovered that, instead of pleasing my Lord and Savior, I turned to pleasing people for the majority of the past 20 years.

As I looked at myself and meditated on the Word of God, the Lord pointed out some crucial things to me. I thought I had been living to serve Him. Instead, I found that I had been living to serve others to gain their approval. I wasn't even doing anything to serve myself!

Long story short, I came to the realization that I needed to *Get Over Myself, Get Out of My OWN Way, so that I could Get What I Wanted Out of Life.*

It has definitely been an incredible journey! Just as when I trained to be a Drill Sergeant in the US Army, I have also trained to be a Drill Sergeant in the Army of Life.

I hope it will not take you as long as it took me to *Get Over Yourself, Get Out of Your OWN Way, and Get What YOU Want Out of Life.*

In the following chapters, you will discover 7 Drill Sergeant of Life-Tips and 7 Clarity Affirmations. These Tips and Affirmations will help you move from being AWOL from the Army of Life and an attendant to the Nuptials of Mediocrity to the real deal: the Bride or Groom at the Wedding Gala of Life.

You will find such Drill Sergeant of Life-Tips as:

- How to move your life from C.R.A.P.P.P.P.Y., make it S.N.A.P.P.P.Y. so you can be H.A.P.P.P.P.P.Y.Y!
- How to S.T.E.P. into your purpose
- How to get to the root of those excuses you keep using
- How to have faith and believe in yourself
- How to F.O.C.U.S.

You will find Affirmations such as:

- I am here <u>for</u> some Body
- I am here <u>for</u> some Thing
- I am here <u>to do</u> great things

If you read and follow the instructions and advice given in this book, (and, I do hope you read the entire book!) you

will experience change! The change will begin on the inside; the most important place to start.

Before you know it, those changes will do amazing things in your life!

As you read this book the first time, underline key points that hit you where it hurts (or feels good.) Then, go back and read it again; you may not get it the first time.

In fact, you may be so upset/angry/putout with yourself and with me, you may throw the book into traffic on the freeway (wishing it was me!)

Please! Get a cup of coffee, tea, water and start again. I promise; you will *Get Over Yourself, Get Out of Your Own Way, and Get What You Want Out of Life!*

You will move forward into the destiny that was created just for you. Before you know it, you will return to being the soldier you were created to be. You will be better equipped for life and start enjoying life more than ever before!

Sounds crazy? Keep reading; you *will* find yourself somewhere in this book.

How To Get Over Yourself, Get Out of Your Own Way, and Get What
YOU Want Out of Life!

PHASE ONE

GET OVER YOURSELF!

1 YOU ARE A SOLDIER...

...Whether you like it or not!

You have just entered Phase One of **Get Over Yourself Boot-Camp.** As far as I am concerned, you have already succeeded: you purchased this book **after** reading the Disclaimer! I am proud of you already!

Life is a battlefield! Every day brings new conflicts and skirmishes. Each day, you put on your battledress uniforms and wade into the sea of humanity. You go from sea to shining sea waging war to get what belongs to you.

Your jobs, businesses, family, and better pay. You fight for what is rightfully yours. You fight to defend your freedom to live as you choose. You fight for your children to have the best you can give them. You fight, fight, fight...

But, some things keep you from winning the battle! What are those things? ...Either you, or others, or both.

You allow many things to conquer you. You become ineffective in waging war against those who keep you from reaching your objective: your purpose and mission in life!

Many of you were, at one time, good soldiers in life. Unfortunately, you have become gun-shy and war weary. Life beat you up so badly, you went AWOL! You now have the attitude,

Que sera sera; whatever will be, will be...

17

You gave up your ground! Now, you are stuck in the background of someone else's life. You suffer from something I call,

The Bridesmaid Syndrome.

You have martyred all of your hopes, dreams and desires. You gave up on the life and purpose you were supposed to have. You have taken service to others to a whole other level!

You see, in dealing with self, we all have a cross to bear. Not only should we be aware and careful of the image we project to others, we should especially take care of the image we project to ourselves. If we lean toward a poor self-image, others lean toward that same image and treat us in like manner.

In church, you were probably taught that anything to do with self is wrong, especially if you tend to sway toward narcissism. However, the Bible also says that you are to love God with all your heart, mind, and strength. You are also to love your neighbors *as* you love yourself.

The only way you can accomplish this feat, though, is by having a positive self-image. You have to love yourself *before* you can even hope to love someone else (even God.) You have to treat others the way you want to be treated.

You need to change the view you have of yourself so you can help others view you in a different light. If you continually see yourself as only a Bridesmaid in life, how can anyone else ever view you as a Bride?

Life has horrifically beat up on many of you precious folks causing you to consistently fall into lesser roles. Why? You believe it is the only place for you in life.

NOT TRUE!!!

Believe it or not, for years I found myself in the same predicament! Yes, even after serving as a Drill Sergeant I found myself as **always** the Bridesmaid and **never** the Bride in practically every phase of my life.

I always assisted others in their role as Bride or Groom. I just never made it out of the starting box to be the Bride myself.

Finally, FINALLY, I have stepped into my rightful place as the Bride... **AND IT IS FUN!** It is the place I am supposed to be. And I am here to help **YOU** do the same.

There is one thing you must understand about the Army of Life: you have the same opportunities and chances as anyone else to make it to the top. Although at times it may seem otherwise, this is a true statement.

You have the opportunity to fight against your enemies both foreign (outside of yourself) and domestic (your inner man.) You have the authority to seize your enemies and take away their power. You also have the power to overcome obstacles placed before you.

For God hath not given us the spirit of fear; but of power, and of love, and of a sound mind. (II Timothy 1:7)

The Bridesmaid Syndrome is a definitive enemy to your freedom, growth, and purpose. It is a constant invader of civil liberties and a very real foe that needs to be fought against.

Folks affected by the Bridesmaid Syndrome contend with:

Self-defeat	Negative Self-talk
Martyrdom	Negative Self-image
"Yes" Mentality	Unworthiness
Low Self-Esteem	No love for self
People Pleasing	Being Untrue to self

At some point in your life, you need to fight your way out of the Nuptials of Mediocrity and into the Wedding Gala of Excellence. You need to gain the ground that mediocrity has stolen from you.

You are here for so much more!

At your creation, you were destined for something a great deal more extraordinary than a simple assignment as a Bridesmaid or Groomsman. God Almighty, the God of Abraham, Isaac and Jacob – the God of the Holy Scriptures - had a higher plan for you.

It is your time and season to come back to the purpose you were created for. But, you have to want it! I can prepare the material for you; but you have to read it. I can instruct and mentor you in the direction you need to take; but, you must travel the road.

Keep reading; the best is yet to come!

2 IT'S NOT ABOUT YOU!

Somewhere, someone is searching for you. Trust me; it's true.

You see, we expected someone like Michael Jackson to make an appearance in our lives. We had experienced the Elvises, the Dean Martins, the Frank Sinatras, and the Nat King Coles. We needed an honest-to-goodness, identifiable icon the Baby Boomer Generation could recognize. And we got just what we wanted!

In 1958, the world had no idea that a mega-superstar would soon be born. Sure, many babies were born in 1958, January 1 through December 31. But, around November 1957, the stars lined up in the heavens. A mega-superstar was conceived.

Almighty God paid special attention (as He always does.) This was the moment He waited for: to send one of His special beings to the Earth. He may have even said,

This Is It!

Now, don't get me wrong; we are all special in some way or the other. Each of us has a gift or talent differing from other gifts and talents in our sphere of influence. Each of us is special to our parents and the families we are born into.

But, every once in a while, an exceptional person comes along; one who puts the world on notice. A person using everything he or she is endowed with in their psyche to make an uncommon mark on the world.

Michael Jackson was one such exceptional person.

Now, this book is by no means about Michael Jackson or any of the other characters I mention throughout. No, this book is about how **you** can *Get Over Yourself and Get What You Want Out of Life!*

Believe it or not, Michael Jackson got over himself to become the superstar, MEGA superstar, he was. As a child and throughout most of his adult life, Michael Jackson was exceedingly shy.

He didn't hang out in public much. Wherever he went, crowds flocked to him. He didn't have a lot to say and led a very private life.

But, when he stepped on-stage... His entire personality changed. He became a super-self who popped, locked, and moon-walked into our homes and hearts. Michael Jackson experienced iconic status few others could ever imitate or reach.

Almighty God planned this event with great care. He knew that the family He assigned Michael to expected a shining star who would catapult their family to music celebrity. Joseph and Katherine Jackson were prepared to nurture the one God would send into their midst. And nurture they did!

Maybe, at some point in time after Michael's conception, Joseph and Katherine realized there was something different, maybe exceptional, about this particular pregnancy; they just didn't know what it was! But they expected something, some One great!

The same goes for you. Someone waits for your appearance in their lives. This person does not know your name, your birth date, what you look like, where you live or anything else pertinent about you. As a matter of fact, this person doesn't even realize he or she is searching for you.

You have a word for this person. A smile. A hug. A... something.

The world has prepped itself just for you. So, you see, it's not about you. You were not born for you! You were born for what you would bring into the world and into the lives of the people you encounter.

Your parents wanted a little bundle of joy: They were given You.

Your siblings needed someone who could be blamed for everything: It was You!

Your kindergarten teacher expected one to either cross the line and be sent to the principal's office consistently or make everyone proud that he or she had come into their lives: YOU!

Honestly, it is not by sheer coincidence you are here. **You are here _for_ some Body.**

Go ahead; try that thought on for size. Say it out loud:

I am here _for_ some Body!

This book was written so that you, my faithful reader and friend, will be able to **Get Over Yourself, Get Out of Your Own Way, and Get What YOU Want Out of Life** enjoying a more fulfilling existence than ever before.

You see, right now many of you reading this book are leading very C.R.A.P^5.Y. lives and don't understand why.

In other words, you **C**an't **R**eally **A**chieve your **P**otential because you (and those around you) continually **P**unish, **P**enalize, **P**ersecute, or **P**ut **Y**ou(rself) down.

There's no need to fear; the Drill Sergeant of Life is here!

I will show you how the "Bridesmaid Syndrome" causes you to live a C.R.A.P^5.Y. life. By the end of this book, you will be **empowered** to make it S.N.A.P^3.Y. and move from C.R.A.P^5.Y. to H.A.P^5.Y^2.

Let's get started.

For many years, I have always laughed about, yet commiserated with others, over the phrase, "**Always** the Bridesmaid, **never** the Bride."

Recently, while penning this book, I meditated more on the deeper meaning and ramifications of this saying.

Always the Bridesmaid, Never the Bride.

Think about it: a person continually seeing her or himself as **always** a Bridesmaid or Groomsman in life **always** sees her or himself as second best. They **never** see themselves as able to rise to the status of Bride or Groom.

Always being the Bridesmaid or Groomsman contributes greatly to one leading a C.R.A.P⁵.Y. life.

You **C**an't **R**eally **A**chieve your full **P**otential because you **always P**unish, **P**enalize, **P**ersecute or **P**ut **Y**ourself down!

Now, please, hang in there with me as I expand on this wonderful metaphor. This is life we are talking about. You are here **for** some Body: To accomplish great things in that person's life. How can you do that if you **always** see yourself as second best?

You are a key player in the lives of the people you were created to impact. You are not placed on the sidelines; you are in the thick of things! But first, you need to ***Get Over Yourself and Get Out of Your Own Way!***

You want to be the Bride, don't you? The Groom, I'll betcha! That's what you are here for!

Think about the career Bridesmaid: **always** participating in dozens of weddings but **never** as the main attraction. Consider the professional Groomsman: **always** asked to stand as the second-best but **never the** Best man? (After all, isn't the groom the best man for the bride?)

At some point or the other, the Bridesmaid or the Groomsman eventually asks him or herself,

Why hasn't some One ever wanted ME to be the Bride or the Groom? Why haven't I found my perfect match?

Let's look at the Ps of this acronym for a moment:

Potential – Existing only as a possibility and not in fact; possible. You have the *potential* to be anything in life you want. You have the *potential* to be the Bride or the Groom. It is up to you whether you, in fact, rise up to the incredible *potential* you have inside! And yes, my friend, you have a question, don't you?

How do I find that potential, Beatrice?

First of all, stop looking at who you are. Instead, look at who you can and will be if you will **Get Over Yourself.**

Secondly, allow yourself to dream again of all the possibilities available to you. It's not too late for anything to occur in your life.

I don't want to get ahead of the book, but think of this: What do people always find most useful about you? What skill do you have that others continually desire to exploit and use on their behalf? In the next chapter, you will find a questionnaire that will assist you in finding your potential and purpose.

Punish/**P**enalize – To inflict a penalty for a fault or crime; castigate (too close to castrate for me!), correct, discipline. We punish ourselves when we constantly diminish our joy because of perceived faults or crimes.

I messed up when I was younger. Now that I am older, I don't deserve to have anything good happen in my life! I don't deserve to be the Bride/Groom!

Another question, perhaps?

Beatrice, how do I get over my past to see or be my future?

It is essential that you **want** to let go of your past. If you continually drive while looking in the rearview mirror, what do you think will eventually happen? You will wreck your car, won't you? Well, if you continually look in the rearview mirror of life, you won't be able to see yourself going forward. Instead of concentrating on what's coming, you only concentrate on what's behind you.

When you look in the mirror, you don't see who you were, you see who you are. In the mirror of your mind, though, you can also see who you can be. God the Creator, sees you as who you are going to be; you are constantly evolving as He brings you into different seasons of life. You have a bright future ahead of you! God wants you to move forward and not hold yourself back in the past. Stop punishing yourself for what you did and focus on what you are doing and going to do!

The Drill Sergeant of Life says: *Get Over Yourself and Move Forward!*

Persecute – To disturb the peace of mind especially by repeated disagreeable acts; afflict; irritate. Let's face it: no one wants you to fail as much as those who (supposedly) wish you well! Because of the negative image you sometimes portray, others expect you to fail. Believe it or not, you expect yourself to fail!

If you choose to do that, I will not support you!

I will not get any support from anyone because I fail all the time!

Let's face it: misery loves company. So do doubt, confusion, and unbelief. But, you do not have to be the one keeping them company! Move forward out of and away from persecution. Allow yourself to recognize persecution **before** it knocks on the door of your life. You have a choice.

Put-down - An act or expression showing scorn and usually intended to hurt another's feelings; insult. The act of making a person or a thing seem little or unimportant; depreciation.

Honey, you're not good enough to be a Bride/Groom/ Manager/Business Owner/Singer, etc. You will never be as good as so-and-so! You may as well stay right where you are so you won't get out there and fail... Again!

Now I know you have a really burning question at this point.

How do I raise my self-esteem, Beatrice? I have been so beat up and put down that I can't even raise my head any more.

Look in the mirror; we're going to do a little self-talk here. No; really. Look in the mirror.

The Drill Sergeant of Life says, Repeat after me:

I, (state your name,) am better than what others think I am.

I, (state your name,) am better than what I think I am.

I am smarter. I am brighter.

I am created to do the impossible and the improbable.

Some Body is expecting me. This person expects me to be a catalyst of change in their life.

I AM HERE FOR SOME BODY AND I AM THE CATALYST OF CHANGE FOR THEIR LIFE.

How does that make you feel? Repeat this encouragement several times throughout your day. Say it with feeling; say it with power! Allow the words to invoke strong emotion within until you walk with confidence and a new sense of purpose in your life.

You were not created to lead a C.R.A.P⁵.Y. life! You were not created or sent here for some Body to fulfill **their** deepest desires by *helping* you lead a C.R.A.P⁵.Y. life.

Before and during the wedding celebration, the job of everyone involved is to cater to the happy (for the most part) couple.

Mostly though, all the catering is done for the benefit of the Bride because, *if the Bride isn't happy…* Well, you know the rest.

Anyway, when a Bridesmaid steps out of place (after all, it's not about you!) the bride seeks swift vengeance:

*You **CAN** be replaced!*

Likewise, the Groomsman. As a matter of fact, any slight or sign of disloyalty can be taken out on the basketball court in this fashion:

Man, I TOLD you (as he slams the ball into his errant partner's face) *I would get you back for messing up my wedding! She harped on your mistake the entire HONEYMOON!!!* (dunking the ball on the Groomsman's head again!*)*

These scenarios leave the Bridesmaid and Groomsman feeling whipped, defeated, as though they serve only one purpose in life: to serve the monsters they previously called a friend.

Now, of course, after all the festivities, the honeymoon, and everything has settled down or returned to semi-normal, the Bride and Groom have certain expectations.

The Bride expects her little Bridesmaid to overlook everything occurring during those anxiety-filled moments leading to the wedding. She wants to be best friends again.

The Groom, of course, expects his best bud to play basketball with no thought to the guerrilla tactics used before.

But, the heart and mind of the frustrated attendant – **YOU** - may have been damaged beyond repair! This conflict and the subsequent browbeating may have happened, perhaps, one time too many! (***See what happens when you forget to be a soldier?***)

You mope for days, licking your wounds, trying to go on with life. You go to work, finding yourself sinking deeper and deeper into the morass of depression.

*Why am I **always** treated like this? I guess I'm no better
than this. I should **never** expect any better because this
continually happens to me. I will **never** be a Bride/
Groom. I will **never** be a CEO/CFO/ Manager,
businesswoman/man. I will **never** be in charge of
anything because I'm just not made for such things. I will
just settle where I am and leave it at that. (*Can you hear
the *Woe is me* in this diatribe?)

STOP!!!!!

Hold on right there!!!!!

GET OVER YOURSELF!!!!!!!

This is not you! **You are here <u>for</u> some Body!**

You are not here for some Body to hurt, degrade,
mistreat, gossip about, or persecute. You are very
valuable to God and to those He created you for. You were
not created to be devalued and made to feel low!

Although you can't always control how others treat you,
you *can* always rise above their (and your own)
expectations. Just as the Bridesmaid can be replaced, so
can the Bride! Don't allow yourself to continually be
treated in such a manner.

Rise above the hurt and anguish others inflict on you with
rarely any thought to do otherwise. Let your feelings be
known with love. Let the perpetrator know that you are
not interested in being treated the way they have decided
to treat you. Let your love shine toward them even if they
show no true love towards you.

You were created to travel on the High Road of Excellence! After turning the other cheek, move on into your purpose and do what you know you were created to do!

Take the High Road of Excellence instead of the Middle Road of Mediocrity or the Low Road of Passivity.

Neither the Bride, nor the Groom, nor anyone else has the right or permission (unless you give it!) to cause you to live a C.R.A.P⁵.Y. life! Next to God Who created you, your life is in **your** hands. **YOU** hold the keys to your success; no one else!

You decide what type of life you live; not someone else!

Remember the title of this chapter? *It's not about you!* That's very true. But, it *is* about how you affect others. It *is* about the way in which you react to the cards you are dealt. You have a choice in **all** the matters of your life.

Not only do others *expect* you to show up in their lives, once you get there, they watch you. They look to you as an example of how they should treat the situations they encounter.

Michael Jackson made mostly good choices in his life. He also made bad choices. One of his best choices was to take what he had been given before he was born – singing, dancing, and stage presence – and turn it into a multimillion dollar industry supplying the needs of his family for all of their lifetimes.

As a Bridesmaid or Groomsman, you serve the needs of the Bride or the Groom to the best of your abilities. You sacrifice many things! But, you should not lose yourself in the process!

You are to help or assist the Bride or Groom in whatever way, shape, form or fashion they need. Your service to them should never decrease your relevance.

Even as you assist the Bride or Groom, *you are still you!* You are still the person you were created to be; **you just need to act like it!**

And HOW do you act like it, you ask? Remember those words of encouragement from earlier? Well, now, it's time to walk that encouragement out in your life.

Believe you are **better than what others think you are.** Know in your heart of hearts that you are **better than you think you are.**

Encourage yourself continually. Repeat good things about yourself. Say things to yourself that you know no one else will say about you except maybe your parent(s), spouse or children. Believe what you proclaim to yourself. Believe that you are here as a **catalyst of change for some Body!**

You have much to offer in all situations. You are here to help! Helping does not mean you are a whipping girl or boy!

GET OVER YOURSELF!

You are here <u>for</u> some Body!

You are here to help Some Body be the best he or she can be.

You are not here to always say, "YES!" just so you won't create any hard feelings. Believe it or not, some folks need to hear "NO!" so they can keep it real!

You are not here to take the Middle Road of Mediocrity or the Low Road of Passivity just because it is the path of least resistance.

Let me tell you about the path of least resistance!

This is the path most people are comfortable on because it is easy; the comfort zone. The comfort zone causes a person to become complacent and lackadaisical. The person who finds him or herself on the path of least resistance is easily overlooked and discounted.

That's not why you are here! You are here to make waves! You are here to splash water into the faces of your sphere of influence causing them to be all they can be, all they dare to be!

You are not a meatball in a pot of spaghetti sauce! You do not look like all the other meatballs. You are here to make a difference to some Body by being the "you" God created you to be.

So...

GET OVER YOURSELF!!!

Get over your C.R.A.P^5.Y. life! And make it S.N.A.P^3.Y.:

Start Now Achieving your Potential by Promoting and
Pushing Yourself! How?

Surround yourself with people who want the same things
from their own lives. Don't be unequally connected with
folks who want nothing out of life; they will drag you
down to their level.

Surround yourself with people who sincerely try to go by
the same criteria as you involving love; love as described
in the Bible in I Corinthians Chapter 13 (more about this
concept later.) If the folks you surround yourself with
don't love wholeheartedly as you do, you will become
jaded and change your definition of love.

Surround yourself with others who are teachable and
coachable. As the dynamics change in your life, these type
people will want the same changes to occur in their lives.
Then, you will be seen as the catalyst of change you were
created to be.

You're not going to get anywhere by being in and having a
C.R.A.P[5].Y. lifestyle. It's not an honorable place to be.
So... GET OUT OF IT!

But, you need to do it now! The longer you wait, the more
time you waste making a decision on whether you really
want to make a change, the harder it is for you to **just do
it!**

As you can tell, I love acronyms. Acronyms take a simple
word and cause it to fulfill its even greater potential by
pushing its definition to the limit.

S.N.A.P.P.P.Y. - **S**tart **N**ow **A**chieving your **P**otential by **P**romoting and **P**ushing **Y**ourself.

Let's face it: sometimes the only one who thinks the best of you is... **You.**

Now, I'm not saying you always have to toot your own horn. However, it does sound better when someone else sings your praises than you praising yourself.

But, *you* need to promote and encourage yourself. *You* need to push yourself harder than anyone else can ever push you. How, you ask again?

Be fierce with yourself: about your potential and about your purpose in life. *You* know exactly where it is you want to go. *You* know exactly what you were created for (more on this later.) *You* know exactly how to get there.

Stop dragging your feet! You can't always be the Bridesmaid, the Groomsman, the kid brother or sister who only has to look cute. **You are here for some Body.**

The *Drill Sergeant of Life says, Repeat after me:*

This is a new season in my life!

I AM the Bride/Groom I was created to be.

I STAND on top of the Wedding Cake of Life!

I FULFILL my potential and purpose!

You need to make it S.N.A.P^3.Y.:

 Start **N**ow **A**chieving your **P**otential by **P**romoting and **P**ushing **Y**ourself!

You may only start with small steps; but, you have to make at least one step. Pretty soon, as you encourage yourself, you will make two steps. Five. Ten.

Next thing you know, you pick up speed. You pass those holding you back. You excel in ways you never thought possible.

You achieve hourly, daily, weekly, and monthly goals as never before. People wonder why you are doing so well. They see a different side of your personality.

You are able to tell them with confidence,

I got over myself and got out of my own way so I could get what I want out of life!

Of course, they look at you strangely. They can't help but notice how you <u>a</u>chieve your <u>p</u>otential as never before because you <u>p</u>romote and <u>p</u>ush <u>y</u>ourself.

You decide that, because **you are here <u>for</u> some Body,** your new encouragement is,

If it is to be, it is up to me!

You decide you **can** make changes in your life for the better!

As time goes by, you discover you have much to offer others. Not only can you benefit your sphere of influence but also your neighborhood, your work section, your church, your social group. You have something to offer because these are the some Bodies *you* were created for!

Doesn't that feel good? Finally, you see a light. It becomes brighter as you **a**chieve your **p**otential by **p**romoting and **p**ushing **y**ourself!

And that's only the beginning!

Happy-ness is not something someone can give to you. Happy-ness is something only you can give to yourself.

The next step in your quest to **Get Over Yourself!** is to make H.A.P^5.Y^2. a part of your everyday life.

OK. This is going to be a long one. I used the letter P until I just got... **HAPPPPPPPYY!!!**

You can **H**arvest **A**bundant **P**rosperity by being **P**assionate, **P**atient, **P**ersistent and **P**urposefully **Y**ielded to **Y**our life.

H.A.P.P.P.P.P.Y.Y!

Now, bear with me. I want the light shining so brightly for you that you are forced to wear sunglasses to bed!

You have planted seeds in the lives of many people. Seeds of love, joy, peace, giving, helping, so forth and so on. Now, when a farmer plants seeds, eventually he knows he will reap a harvest from the seeds he planted.

Back to Mr. Jackson: he planted seeds of joy, happiness, good music, and killer dance moves.

In return, he **H**arvested **A**bundant **P**rosperity. He was **P**assionate about what he did. He **P**atiently trained in choreography and **P**ersistently wrote and sang best-selling songs for nearly 40 years. And he **P**urposefully moved through the ranks of the most iconic musical figures who ever lived and <u>Y</u>ielded to the purpose for which he was created.

PHEW!

Pretty cool, huh? Well, guess what? If you will **Get Over Yourself,** you can also **Get What You Want Out of Life!** in much the same way. But, you need to create H.A.P.P.P.P.P.Y.Y. for your own life.

Look back at the seeds you have sown. As the Bible says, you reap what you sow.

What have you sown? Have they been seeds you would love to receive an abundant harvest from? Or, seeds you wish were never planted?

One thing I learned growing up on a farm in South Carolina: you can always plant something new. And that's a good thing! Start now planting new seeds in your life!

GOOD SEED   **VS**   **BAD SEED**

Excellence	Compassion	Jealousy	Envy
Kindness	Self-worth	Hatred	Bitterness
Love	Courage	Gossip	Lies/Deceit
Helpfulness	Wisdom	Complacency	Low Esteem

When you sow negative seeds, you receive a negative harvest. When you sow seeds not conducive to building yourself up in the purpose you were created for, you reap a harvest that causes you to stay on the path of least resistance.

On this path, you continually **not** achieve what you were created to achieve.

Instead, sow positive seeds. These seeds enable you to live a H.A.P.P.P.P.P.Y.Y. existence. You soon discover your **H**arvest is **A**bundant in **P**rosperity. Your **P**assionate **P**atience and **P**ersistence in **P**ursuing your **P**urpose has caused you to **P**urposefully **Y**ield to **Y**our life.

What you have sown has caused you to be the best example to the Some Body you were created for.

The way in which you use your gifts and talents or allow them to be used determine whether you lead a $C.R.A.P^5.Y.$ or a $H.A.P^5.Y^2.$ lifestyle.

GET OVER YOURSELF! Leave your $C.R.A.P^5.Y.$ lifestyle behind. Don't give permission to others so that you:

Can't

Really

Achieve your

Potential because you are

Punishing, **P**enalizing, **P**ersecuting or **P**utting

Yourself down and allowing others to do the same.

Instead, make it $S.N.A.P^3.Y!$

Start

Now

Achieving your

Potential by

Promoting and Pushing

Yourself on the High Road of Excellence and Destiny you were created to walk on. Don't settle for mediocrity.

Finally, get H.A.P^5.Y^2.!

Harvest

Abundant

Prosperity by

Passionately Pursuing your Purpose with Patience and Persistence as you Purposefully

Yield to Your life that you desire. (Don't tell anyone but I got a bit happy with the Ps!)

Decide to jump from C.R.A.P.P.P.P.P.Y to H.A.P.P.P.P.P.P.Y. so you can get on with an enjoyable life!

OK; hang in there with me as we see what else you are here in the world for!

Drill Sergeant of Life-Tip #1: MOVE FROM C.R.A.P.P.P.P.P.Y.; MAKE IT S.N.A.P.P.P.Y. SO YOU CAN BE H.A.P.P.P.P.P.Y.Y!

Action Steps

- ✓ **Get Over Yourself!** You hold the keys to your life.

- ✓ You are not here to be hurt, degraded, misused, gossiped about or persecuted by anyone in any way. Unfortunately, other folks don't know this.

- ✓ You are not here to be a scapegoat or blamed for other's shortcomings. It's up to you how you react to these things occurring in your life.

- ✓ You are not here to enable, hinder, hurt, or harm anyone in any way. If you do, be the bigger person and rectify the situation. It's OK to say, *I'm sorry!*

- ✓ You are here to cherish and to be cherished; to love and to be loved; to be kind and to be kind to.

- ✓ You are here to encourage and to show the way to those who are discouraged and lost.

Clarity Affirmation #1:

I AM HERE <u>FOR </u>SOME BODY.

To be chosen to occupy the same space as someone else whose life you are to affect is an honor and a privilege. You are here to enhance and make better the lives of those you touch.

3 YOU WERE BORN WITH A PURPOSE

Believe it or not, you are filled with a specific purpose.
Before you burst through the womb of time, before you
were thought of on the Earth, the Lord God Almighty,
Creator of us all, installed specific tasks, duties, and goals
within you.

Before I was born, Almighty God decided I would write
this book for the express purpose of helping **you** find your
true purpose. And look; here we both are!

We are doing our thing! We are destined to do what we do
at this particular time to fulfill our purposes on the earth.

Isn't that exciting?

Isn't it exciting to discover that you *have* a purpose? To
discover why in the world you are *really* here? Have you
always been curious to know why you are *really* here?

As an infant, your purpose was minimal. Your main
function in life, in addition to eating, pooping, crying,
burping and sleeping, consisted of looking cute. And you
did that very well indeed! (As a matter of fact, some of you
are **still** kinda cute!)

You brought joy to your parents, siblings, grandparents,
aunts, uncles, and all those around you. You served your
purpose very well.

Not much changed as you emerged from infancy into
toddler-dom. Your chief occupation still consisted of
looking cute. You continued to eat, poop, cry, burp, and

sleep. Now, though, you were also expected to learn to crawl, walk and, eventually, run. And you did!

Before too long, your parents wished they could either bottle your energy or that you would slow down. If they could have bottled your energy, they could have earned money to replace the things you broke as your marathon legs evolved!

Along with your newly-found independence, you made friends through playgroup, the church nursery, in daycare and in kindergarten. You were one of the sweetest little children!

Your Bridesmaid/Groomsman tendencies showed up while you were still very young: you **always** willingly went along with the group. You **never** made waves! When other children snatched your toys, you simply went and got something else or didn't do anything. No biggy!

This passive attitude followed as you entered the halls of academia. You **never** had much to say because there was **always** someone else with something better to say.

 You **never** felt you deserved better treatment from those you called friend. After all, you were only a Bridesmaid/Groomsman; those you helped were the better people.

(Don't laugh! I remember thinking these same thoughts as a child! No one told me differently!)

You shunned aggressive or loud people. You were neither aggressive nor loud and didn't want to draw attention to yourself. You lived in the shadows of others and enjoyed being in the background. You didn't want to be noticed by or get into trouble with teachers or parents.

When asked, teachers made up good things to say to your parents; no offense, but you just didn't make a splash. Although you **always** made good grades, there was **never** anything exceptional about you.

In middle and high school, you plugged along in a so-so manner. You did everything right just like everyone else. Again, you were just the sweetest little thing!

Always helpful; ready, willing, and able to go with everyone else and assist them in accomplishing their goals. You were already very proficient at your role in the Bridal Party and didn't realize it.

Whenever asked your purpose in life, you **always** gave the same answer:

Oh, I want to help others fulfill their destiny in life.

You said it so many times you finally tricked your mind into believing it!

It sounded so good; so martyr-like!

I want to help others fulfill their destiny in life.

You were on a collision course with Sainthood!

It sounded so good to your ears! Every time you said it, you imagined your parent(s) chests sticking out proudly as they said to whoever listened,

*We are so very proud of Barbara/Sarah /Billy/Sam!
She/He is such a wonderful Bridesmaid/ Groomsman for
everyone!*

As you grew older, your parent(s) continued to want only
the best for you. They never really pushed you to go
higher; they wanted to protect you from failure. Let's face
it: there is no failure in being a Bridesmaid or a
Groomsman; all you do is show up!

 Quite possibly, your parent(s) supported your status of
Bridesmaid/Groomsman because this was the only role
they ever played in their lives. And, bless their hearts,
they supported you with all their might!

After graduation from High School and maybe college,
you continued that same line of reasoning. You continued
to *help others fulfill their destiny* giving no thought to
your destiny or purpose.

To thine ownself be true...

But, you **never** learned to be true to you. You **never** told
anyone your honest feelings... about anything! You **never**
divulged what you felt your true life purpose was. You
never shared your true desires with anyone; not even
yourself! (**Never** is such a long time but you *can* turn it
around!)

To this day, you believe it is **always** safer (and easier) to
do what you believe others want you to do. To you, it is
more important to earn their love, honor and respect than
to fulfill your destiny.

If you take the path you *really* want to take, you feel that no one will respect your decision. You alternate between the Middle Road of Mediocrity and the Low Road of Passivity; it *seems* safer. After all, that's where all your family and friends remain, right?

I've got bad news and worse news for you. Which do you want first?

<u>Bad News</u> – **Get Over Yourself!**

You are constantly surrounded by people who need you for one motive or the other. They need *you* to need *them*! They need your help to make it to their destiny. They need your help for the rest of their lives! Their neediness prevents your going forward into the destiny, the purpose for which you were created.

You also surround yourself with folks who want no more out of life than to just make do and hold on. They need you to be like them: stuck in their own little world not achieving their full and great potential.

Now, mind you, these are good, salt-of-the-earth folks. Deep inside, each of them wants more; they just don't know how to get it. So, let me school you and them:

GET OVER YOURSELF SO YOU CAN GET WHAT YOU WANT OUT OF LIFE!

As long as you allow yourself to be used and manipulated by others, you will continue on the paths of mediocrity and passivity.

As long as you allow others to coddle you or buy into your minimalistic vision, you need not expect anything different happening in your life.

You continue to be used and your hopes, dreams, and desires martyred.

As long as you allow it, others have no problem using your talents. They continue doing what they do (very well I might add!) to further their own dreams so they can get to the place *they* want to be in life.

Why don't **YOU** *use* **YOURSELF** so **YOU** can *Get What YOU Want Out of Life!?!?*

The Drill Sergeant of Life Says: *Get Over Yourself, Bridesmaid/Groomsman!*

Yes, you are supposed to help others but, **You Are Here For** **Some Thing** in exactly the same way others are. OK, we will come back to this. Let's move on for right now.

<u>Worse News</u> – *All I want to do is help others fulfill their destiny.*

GET - OVER - YOURSELF!!!!

This is a copout! This is the easiest way for you to never, ever do anything worthwhile with your life.

I say that with certainty, unfortunately, because I have spent the majority of my adult life doing the same! **And it is not what either of us was created for!**

No offense, but, you are lying to yourself. Go ahead; throw the book against the wall, out the window, into the fireplace if you want. Say it with passion,

Beatrice, how dare you get in my face like this!!!

At this point in my journey, I wanted to do and say the same to myself!

The TRUTH hurts!

As I wrote this book, I became a bit emotional at times. I realized what I had done **to myself!** Many of you know I am telling the truth!

It is very easy to pooh-pooh your true desires. You feel so good helping your friends and that's good enough for you, right? Well, guess what? **It's Not!**

At night, you may get a decent rest every once in a while. Most of the time, though, you stay awake; there seems to be a key element missing in your life.

There is some Thing you do and do well that you honestly want to do. Unfortunately, you occupy your time with the wants, needs, hopes, dreams, and desires of others. You allow them to cast a shadow over the things you want to do!

Your heart breaks every time you think of this Thing you want to do. You know how good you would be at it! But other people and their wants, needs, and desires are more important than you and yours.

You just have to live with the **good feeling** of helping them accomplish what they want. *(Dripping sarcasm here!)*

GET OVER YOURSELF!!!

How many others have said the same while holding in their hearts a burning desire to do something with their lives? Something significant that would rock their world?

If everyone had the same attitude, not very much would be accomplished. Yes, you are here to help others; pay it forward, even. But, you have a purpose. That purpose needs to be fulfilled.

The Drill Sergeant of Life says, Repeat after me:

I AM HERE <u>FOR</u> SOME "THING!"

Every person born on this planet has a divine, definite purpose for which he or she was created. Although there will never be another Michael Jackson, Oral Roberts, or Picasso, others follow in their footprints.

Many have come along and danced and sang just like Michael. Some, like Walt Disney, have also created places for children to enjoy. But, none of these have come into the world through Joseph and Katherine Jackson.

Richard Roberts, the son of Oral Roberts, can *almost* preach and pray like his daddy. He even seems to have the same type of faith that healed many sick people. But, he is *not* the same. He has neither the same character, nor the same outlook, nor has he been through the same fires which purified his daddy so Oral could be presented to and used in the world as he was.

As for Picasso; many have tried to imitate his abstract art. Few have fully comprehended or captured the inner struggles of this classical artist. He left a very distinctive stamp on the world.

And, you are here for some **Thing** in the same way. But, how will you accomplish that Thing if you continue to stand in your own way?

Get Over Yourself!

How long will you allow yourself and others to stand in your way? How long will you allow yourself and others to hinder you accomplishing what you were created for?

What is your purpose? What is it that, even if you were not going to be paid or receive any form of compensation, you would still do? For Free? What is that Thing you were created to do?

Now, don't get me wrong; I will be the first person to help someone else. I have done that all of my life. I love helping people. But, I also have a purpose.

My main purpose, right now, in this season, is to help you find your purpose. I fulfill that part of my destiny by speaking and writing to help you find the direction you are intended to travel.

Now, I never said finding your destiny would be easy.

After leaving the military, it took me almost 20 years to come to the startling (*said with much sarcasm!*) conclusion that I love talking and writing. During those

20 years, I searched high and low to find my purpose: it was staring at me the entire time!

I spoke and wrote all the time; it just didn't _seem_ right. I lacked confidence in moving forward in an area I actually excelled in.

While serving in the Army, I was repeatedly assigned to speak to groups of other soldiers (and sometimes civilians) in training-type settings. I wrote technical regulations and manuals. One of my many varied duties was assisting commissioned officers with writing evaluation reports (my reports were always much better!)

As a Drill Sergeant, on any given day of the week, Monday through Saturday, I normally trained 25 – 300 soldiers in various areas of basic combat training during eight-week periods. I was very successful as a trainer.

However, upon leaving the military to focus on raising my family with my husband, I lost sight of my purpose. Even though ingrained in me since before I could remember, I lost something as I made the transition from soldier to housewife. A little of it came back after I was ordained and served as a Pastor for a season.

I loved speaking before groups of people, in this case a congregation. I enjoyed composing sermons and absolutely loved creating Bible Studies and quizzes. I even created puzzles for children.

I wrote Christian plays, songs, and other things. I enjoyed my work in my vocation as a minister. I just never believed I could use that same gifting as a professional speaker and actually make a living doing it!

I was equally good at helping others realize their Thing. I organized ministries and helped pastors excel but lost the zeal to do it for myself. I organized and edited monthly newsletters for church groups but never thought to do one for myself.

It never occurred to me to push myself out there to do what I was created to do.

So, you see, in order for me to tell you how to **Get Over Yourself** and help you do the same, I, first, had to **Get over Myself**. It is definitely an ongoing process.

When you follow the guidance in this book, you will leave your C.R.A.P^5.Y. lifestyle behind and ultimately reach your H.A.P^5.Y^2. place. The enclosed commonsense Tips and Affirmations can easily be used in your daily life. But, these Tips and Affirmations will only work if you apply them!

First things first; you need to discover your true purpose. Although not entirely easy, it is not as difficult as some may think.

Let's make this simple. When you think of a can opener, what images pop into your mind? Popcorn? An orange? A cup of coffee? A gallon jug of milk? If you answered yes to these items popping into your mind at the thought of a can opener, I can't help you. Honestly!

But, if you pictured a can of chicken noodle soup, a pot, or a stove to heat the soup or something similar, we are headed in a good direction.

A can opener was created to… wait for it… **Open cans!**
Now, some of the more sophisticated models may have
bottle openers shaped on the end. There are even multi-
functional can openers that incorporate corkscrews and
knife sharpeners. But, the main purpose for the can
opener is to open cans.

What is your main purpose? The primary **Thing** you were
created to do? Don't get me wrong: there may be more
than one thing you were created to do.

Sometimes this Thing is blatant.

As a child, at the age of nine, I wanted a typewriter for
Christmas; that's all. I wanted to type and create stories;
nothing else. I have followed that desire for most of my
life with writing.

I was also a very good talker. My uncle once informed me
I had the gift of gab and should be a lawyer. (*I'm still
trying to figure out if that was a compliment or an insult!*)
But here I am, speaking and training others because I
love to talk.

So, those are my main purposes in life. Almighty God
instilled in me the gifts and talents making writing and
speaking my foremost Things in life. These two traits
have served me well so far.

But, what is your purpose? What is that **Thing** you like
doing most out of all the other things you have done in
your life? In order to *Get Over Yourself, Get Out of
Your Own Way, and Get What You Want Out of Life*,
you must know beyond a shadow of a doubt what that
Thing is.

So, let's get started. Following is a questionnaire; answer each question as honestly as you can. Now, I warn you: some of the answers will evoke an emotional response. Some of them will make you downright angry. It's OK.

In order for you to find your purpose, your passion, you will have to become emotional. Plug on and wade through those emotions so you can get to the place you need to be: your destiny and purpose.

OK. Ready? Let's go! Take your time; dig deep. Truthfully answer each question. Give each question or statement some thought. When you finish, go back and make note of the questions or statements that really elicited an emotional response. If you complete the questionnaire in one day, leave it for a day or two, go back and review.

My desire is for you to get what YOU want out of life. I believe in you. I don't want **Always** a Bridesmaid/Groomsman; **Never** a Bride/Groom to be a part of your life!

You were born with a purpose. God created you with a specific set of tasks, duties, and goals. Your job is to discover that purpose and S.E.T. it within your heart and mind so you can fulfill your destiny.

You are special! You are here <u>for</u> some Body! You are here <u>for</u> some Thing!

This questionnaire is only a first step in determining your true purpose in life. There are many ways to get there for many different types of people: work-study, entrepreneurship, apprenticeship, etc.

My purpose is to help **you** find **your** way and help you determine your purpose so you can follow the destiny you were created for.

However, you are going to have to **Get Over Yourself!** Allow yourself to do what needs to be done to find your purpose.

Think about it this way; although there are thousands of new inventions created every day of the year, there are still more inventions to be created. By you, perhaps.

Among the hundreds of thousands of books published around the world every year, there is still room for another J. D. Robb, Danielle Steele, John Grisham, Brad Thor or James Patterson. Someone like… You!

You are here for a reason. Almighty God has equipped you, (Yes! YOU!) with particular gifts and talents. He wants you to use them to contribute to the society we live in.

There's a painting to be created…

… a building to be built.

… a recipe to be discovered.

… a song to be sung Joe Sabah says.

The Drill Sergeant of Life says, Come on; say it with me:

I AM HERE <u>FOR </u>SOME THING! I'm not quite sure what it is but it is my time to figure it out!

FINDING MY PURPOSE QUESTIONNAIRE

CHILDHOOD

1. What was your favorite thing to do as a child? Why?

_____

_____

_____

_____

_____

_____

_____

_____

_____

_____

2. What was the main activity your parent(s) had to tell you to stop doing to go to bed most/every night(s)?

_____

_____

_____

_____

_____

_____

_____

_____

_____

3. What role-playing games did you enjoy playing as a child? I.e., teaching your pets, singing with a comb-microphone, styling your doll's hair, etc.

4. What book characters do you remember and
    identify with most from your childhood? Why

5. What did you want to be when you grew up?
    Why?

FINDING MY PURPOSE QUESTIONNAIRE

MIDDLE/JUNIOR/HIGH SCHOOL

1. What subjects did you excel in? Why?

2. What type people were you drawn to and were drawn to you? Why?

_____
_____
_____

3. What sports or other extracurricular activities
   did you participate in? Why? Which gave you the
   greatest pleasure? Why?

_____
_____
_____
_____
_____
_____
_____
_____
_____

4. Who was your favorite role-model in High
   School? Why?

_____
_____
_____
_____
_____
_____
_____
_____
_____

5. From career search evaluations you participated
   in, what was your most likely career following
   High School and College?

_____
_____
_____
_____
_____
_____
_____
_____
_____
_____
_____

6. What was your first job in high school? What did
   you like about it?

_____
_____
_____
_____
_____
_____
_____
_____
_____

7. What were your plans after high school?
   College? Military? Job Corp?

_____
_____
_____
_____
_____
_____

_____
_____
_____
_____

FINDING MY PURPOSE QUESTIONNAIRE

COLLEGE YEARS/MILITARY

1. If you went to college, what was the burning desire that sent you there? Why?

_____
_____
_____
_____
_____
_____
_____
_____
_____

2. What did you major or minor in? Was this your choice or the choice of your parents, guardian, or mentor? Why?

_____
_____
_____
_____
_____
_____
_____
_____

3. What did you do with that major or minor? Why?

_____

_____

_____

_____

_____

_____

_____

_____

_____

_____

4. Are you currently working in the field of your studies? Are you enjoying yourself? Why? Why not?

_____

_____

_____

_____

_____

_____

_____

_____

_____

5. If you opted for the military, what was your specialty?

_____

_____

_____

_____
_____
_____
_____
_____
_____
_____

6. Are you currently working in your specialty or field of study? Are you enjoying yourself? Why? Why not?

_____
_____
_____
_____
_____
_____
_____
_____

FINDING MY PURPOSE QUESTIONNAIRE

PRESENT DAY

1. Do you feel that your life is over and it is too late to change the dynamics in your life? Why?

_____
_____
_____
_____
_____

_____

_____

_____

_____

2. What is your current occupation? Are you **honestly** enjoying yourself?

_____

_____

_____

_____

_____

_____

_____

_____

_____

3. What is the burning desire for your life right now? Why?

_____

_____

_____

_____

_____

_____

_____

_____

_____

_____

4. What do you love to do that causes you to lose track of time? Why?

_____
_____
_____
_____
_____
_____
_____
_____
_____
_____

5. What gift or talent do most people come to you
   for and compliment you on?

_____
_____
_____
_____
_____
_____
_____
_____
_____

6. What do you think about doing most? Why?
   Would you do it for free? (FOCUS, PEOPLE!)

_____
_____
_____
_____
_____
_____
_____

7. How much time, effort, money are you willing to
    spend on fulfilling your purpose

_____

_____

_____

_____

_____

_____

_____

_____

_____

_____

8. How important is it to you to fulfill your purpose
    in life?

_____

_____

_____

_____

_____

_____

_____

_____

_____

_____

9. Are you ready to change the dynamic in your
    life? Why? Why Not?

_____

_____

10. What do you see for your life right now?

11. After you **Get Over Yourself,** where do you see
    yourself within the next year? Three years? Five
    Years?

12. **Bonus Question to think about: If you knew what your last day to live life would be, what would be the first thing you would do? (Quit your job, go on vacation, etc.)**

_____

_____

_____

_____

_____

_____

_____

_____

_____

Drill Sergeant of Life-Tip #2 – S.T.E.P. INTO YOUR PURPOSE

Action Steps

- **SEARCH** for your purpose as though it were a lost $100 bill or diamond ring! Your purpose is one of the most important assets in your life. Treat it as such!
- **TARGET** your purpose. Once you discover your purpose, target it and diminish everything else that does not produce successful fulfillment. Replace actions or events with tasks and goals designed to help you accomplish your purpose.
- **ENGAGE** your purpose every day. Do things that cause you to become proficient in your true purpose. You may have to take baby steps at first. As you engage your purpose more, you will soon take giant leaps in fulfilling your purpose and destiny.
- **PROCEED** with your purpose. Pull out all the stops and proceed with confidence, some caution, and much courage as you move forward.

Clarity Affirmation #2

I AM HERE FOR SOME THING!

Because I am here for some Thing, I expect doors to open that were previously closed. As I walk through these doors into my purpose, I become more experienced and confident as I exercise my ability to achieve all I set out to achieve.

PHASE TWO

GET OUT OF YOUR OWN WAY

4 THE PARADOX

You have now entered **Phase Two** of *Get Over Yourself Boot-Camp!* You made it through Phase One! I am so proud of you! I knew you could do it! Let's jump right in, shall we?

Your life is a paradox. There are certain qualities or features that seem to conflict with one another; contradiction.

Conflict is all around you! Believe it or not, most of your conflict is within! In many aspects of life, you are double-minded. Your heart and mind says:

I want to be the Bride/Groom.

I want to build a business for my family and me.

I want to be the CEO of an international business/ministry.

Unfortunately, your actions, words, and deeds say:

I will NEVER be the Bride/Groom because what I am living right now is my lot in life.

I am not smart enough to do anything other than what I am doing right now!

I will ALWAYS be stuck right where I am!

Your desire is to do great things in your lifetime and to have many wonderful accomplishments. However, know this; it is not enough to just *desire* anything. Your desires need to work in conjunction with action. Action moves you forward into your purpose. You *will* **Always** be a Bridesmaid if you **Never** put forth the effort to be a Bride!

Although you *desire* with all your heart to be the Bride or the Groom, until you put definitive action with your desire, you will always find yourself in the place in which you put your hopes, dreams, and desires on the back burner.

I know the next question:

Beatrice, what are some of the definitive actions I need to put into play?

If you desire to be a Bride or a Groom, your actions need to be complete and thorough. You need to show others that you intend to be the Bride or the Groom by whatever means necessary!

Consider the following example for every aspect of your life whether personal or business.

Men, in order to be a groom, you need to find a nice young lady who is willing to be your bride. Now, I can't tell you where to find this nice young lady but I've heard that the club is not the place. (Ladies, pay attention!)

So, say you join a singles group at your local church or community center? You now have the opportunity to meet many new faces; perhaps your Lady-Love will be there. This is only the beginning. The first one you meet may not be the one for you. You may have to pay your dues and really search for your future bride and mother of your children.

So, say you find an acceptable candidate. Now, you go about the process of getting to know your prospective wife. This will not happen over-night. It may take months; it may take years. If she is the right one for you, time will not matter as much as getting to know everything there is to know about her.

What is her favorite restaurant and meal? Where would she like to live? How many children does she want? You have a ton of fun as you both learn new things about the other.

Then, you make the most life-changing decision you have ever made: after months, maybe years of getting to know each other, you decide that you love this woman and want to spend the rest of your life with her. You propose! Congratulations!

You've done your due diligence and purchased the perfect accessory for the occasion: the RING! You purchase the one that will give you the results you desire!

Next, you find a romantic spot to take your prospective bride. Maybe you take her to the place you went on your first date; or, a family gathering; or, to a church event. You have any number of places in which you can ask that most important question. You ask the question on bended knee and, guess what? She says,

YES!!!

OK, you are on a roll! It's time to prepare for the nuptials. You and your intended set the date, the location, your entourage, receive counseling from your minister, decide what to wear; all the fun stuff. The date looms before you. You are more nervous now than when you asked the question!

Finally, the day arrives and goes off without a hitch. You and your beautiful Bride are off to parts unknown for your honeymoon and to start your lives together. Isn't that wonderful? Finally the Bride! Finally the Groom!

Had you not placed these definitive actions into play first, this day would not have occurred. When you don't couple definitive actions with your desires, you end up standing at the altar alone. Your inaction is indicative of your placing more favor on the hopes, dreams, and desires of others. Why? Because you feel that their hopes, dreams, and desires are more important than your own.

The Drill Sergeant of Life says: Get Out of Your Own Way!

In order to be the Bride or the Groom, you must change the dynamic of the old saying,

Always a Bridesmaid; Never a Bride.

How about,

Sometimes a Bridesmaid; But Also a Bride.

Or,

Frequently a Bridesmaid; But I'm Next!

At some point, each of us desires to serve as the Bride or the Groom. We want to go on the honeymoon. We want others to celebrate us. This is where the paradox prevails: we continue to allow ourselves to always think that we are only worthy to serve as the Bridesmaid or Groomsman. We accept the idea that this has become our lot.

Now, I use the terms Bridesmaid and Groomsman as metaphors for life. It can be used in every aspect of your life. Rest assured: there is nothing, absolutely nothing wrong with being a Bridesmaid or Groomsman every once in a while. This is the tone we set as we allow ourselves to operate or be used in all of life's circumstances.

The Bible says in Galatians 6:9, *And let us not be weary in well doing; for in due season, we shall reap if we faint not.*

As you continue serving as a Bridesmaid or Groomsman throughout your life, you need to determine if you are *well* doing or *ill* doing. Well doing brings a reward of reaping what we have sown (which is good if we have sown good seed!) However, ill doing only brings a harvest of rotten produce if we are not careful.

Although there is nothing wrong with serving in this capacity many times over, we also need to get out of the mindset of...

Always a Bridesmaid, never a Bride...

Always an associate, never a partner...

Always a secretary, never an executive...

You see, in actuality, the Bridesmaid or Groomsman always stands beside; never in front of or on top. When you picture the wedding cake, you only see two people; the Bride and Groom. The wedding is for the Bride and Groom. The honeymoon is **ONLY** for the Bride and Groom!

Well, *the Drill Sergeant says:* **It's time for YOUR wedding!**

This is your season to be the Bride or the Groom; nothing less! I am here to help you be the best Bride or Groom you can possibly be.

OK, I know my Christian brothers and sisters are probably saying,

Well, Beatrice, the Bible says that...

the first shall be last and the last shall be first. It also says that...

he that shall be greatest of all must be a servant of all. And don't forget to...

bear one another's burdens and so fulfill the law of Christ!

To which I say:

Amen! Amen! Amen!

Yes, the Bible says all this and more about serving. The Bible also says that if we follow and keep the commandments of the Lord, He will make us the **HEAD** and not the **TAIL; ABOVE ONLY** and not **BENEATH!**

If we keep God's commandments for our lives, we will not always serve as the Bridesmaid or Groomsman; we will certainly be the Bride or the Groom.

Michael Jackson was destined to be a Groomsman with The Jackson Five for only a limited amount of time. He was destined to serve as the Groom for the majority of his musical career. As we well know, he stood on top of the Wedding Cake of Life!

Think about this statement:

Mediocrity and laziness are mindsets. So is Greatness.

These actions (or inactions) are ingrained in our minds in either negative or positive ways.

For example, look at laziness. As human beings, it is essential that we have set times of rest and relaxation. This prevents becoming over-worked or stressed out. That's a good thing.

But, always chilling out and maxing and relaxing becomes laziness when a person procrastinates. He or she neglects doing what he or she needs to do when he or she needs to do it.

The educational system provides frequent periods of rest and relaxation for its students. During each school day, students have study hall, recess, and lunch. Not to mention field trips and teacher-only days.

When a student takes constant "lunch breaks" during important class time, he or she is classified as lazy. Why? Even though his or her brain is strong and capable enough to complete the course work, this organ takes a holiday at the most inappropriate time. At that time, the brain refuses to do anything but remain in the rest mode.

The Bridesmaid Syndrome causes one to have a lazy or mediocre mindset as well. The person who stays in this position refuses to move forward as a Bride or Groom. He or she *always* experiences being unfulfilled and *never* realizes his or her destiny. This inadvertently brings conflict into his or her life.

Know this: you will not have an easy time breaking free from the Bridesmaid Syndrome. In your quest to *Get Over Yourself, Get Out of Your Own Way,* and *Get What YOU Want Out of Life,* you will go up against one of the most hostile military factions ever: **YOURSELF!**

During your quest, you are forced to overcome the learned behavior you have operated with for so long. While changing your mind and view of yourself, you find more things that *need* to change. These actions also cause conflicts within. These conflicts are much worse than any you will encounter from without!

You see, **you were created to do great things**. Not middle or low-road stuff either. There is a purpose inside you that can cause you to do greater things than you ever dreamed possible.

But, instead of doing great things, you have either played the role of Bridesmaid or Groomsman or you have told yourself these fated words,

I can't do it!

I can't find a Bride!

I can't find the right business for me!

I can't write this book!

Many people have been instrumental in helping you fulfill the implications behind these thoughts. They have been quite helpful in causing you to not be able to do what you set out to do!

Many Naysayers and Discouragers have invaded your life. These sweet folk have decided that their way is the best way for you.

They (and I will not say they are well-meaning either) continually attempt (successfully I might add) to mold and shape you into *their* idea of the perfect you. Never mind they shape you into what and who *they* want to be, do or have in *their* lives.

Joseph Jackson, the Jackson patriarch, desired to see his five sons onstage as the Jackson Five. They were ultra successful for many years. I don't know when it happened, but, at some point, Michael wanted more.

He loved singing with his brothers. He enjoyed performing on the world's stages with them. But, he wanted to step out of the wedding party and become the Groom instead of a Groomsman.

Do you remember what happened after the Jackson Five split up?

First, there was *The Jacksons*. Then, the other brothers attempted to launch their solo careers. Out of the four older brothers, Jermaine was probably the most successful even though his solo career was short-lived.

The four eldest brothers eventually recruited younger brother Randy to continue the Jackson Five legacy. This move failed also.

Michael, however, went on to bigger and better things. He went out and found his Bride! By the time *Thriller* appeared, he was known as one of the world's greatest entertainers. But, he had to step out of the shadow of the group to become the mega-star we knew and loved.

Michael never seemed like someone who ever said to himself,

I can't.

I cannot imagine him saying,

I can't do this dance step.

I can't go on that stage.

I can't sing that note!

Instead, he probably said things like,

How can I learn to do that? Who can I find to teach me?

Throughout his career, Michael Jackson seemed to have a good perspective of himself. That perspective moved him forward from mediocre to exceptional in life.

Instead of telling yourself you *can't* do something, change your mind-set! See the possibility and the probability in everything you do.

It is probable. Better yet: **It is possible!**

You cannot allow other's views to dictate how and what you think of yourself. You can't allow Naysayers and Unbelievers to color the way you see your world. You can't allow them to hinder your accomplishments.

The Drill Sergeant of Life says, Repeat after me:

I am here to do GREAT things!

Express this with passion! You see, as soon as you say it, a little voice in the back of your mind says the opposite,

I am just here by coincidence, not for anything special.

I will never accomplish anything worthwhile in my lifetime.

Train your mind to accept this concept. How?

Create post-it notes with good things about yourself. Post these notes on your mirrors, doors, ceiling over your bed, car mirrors, dashboards, and computer monitor. Post them anywhere else you can think to constantly remind you throughout the day that:

- **I am Here <u>for</u> some Body.**
- **I am Here <u>for </u>some Thing.**
- **I am Here <u>to do</u> GREAT things!**

Pretty soon, you will find that you are picking your head up, throwing your shoulders back and your chest out proclaiming,

I MOST CERTAINLY CAN!

Doesn't that feel good? Doesn't that give you a better perspective of yourself?

You can now picture yourself in that $20,000 wedding gown, can't you? Gentlemen, you can now see yourself in that tuxedo with top-hat and tails, waiting at the altar for your Lady-Love, right? The way you are dressed now is much better than that toned-down (mostly ugly) Bridesmaid or Groomsman outfit, isn't it?

It's only a matter of adjusting your personal perspective and the tasks in front of you. It's about your attitude. And attitude is everything!

Think about your last great success.

How much time has elapsed between that event and now? What obstacles did you cross in order to succeed then? What negative things were said about you or you said about yourself? How did you feel when you experienced that success?

These are questions to ask yourself over and over again as you set yourself up to experience more successes. After all, **you are here to do great things!** Those great things are successful events in your life.

Now, of course, one *can* experience great big messes in life as well. But, we are not talking about great big messes.

We are talking about huge successes resulting in you making an enormous mark on society.

The Drill Sergeant of Life says: *GET OUT OF YOUR OWN WAY!*

Inhale success! Exhale failure, doubt, unbelief, discouragement and other negatives clogging your success system. From now on, breathe an entirely different way than before.

Sniff out opportunities that will lead to your greatest successes. Join networking groups so you can meet others who are already successful. Put your best foot forward at all times! Be assured that you are walking through the right door at the right time.

It is essential to keep divine appointments with the right situation. Doing this causes you to land on top where you are supposed to be. How can you tell if it is a divine appointment?

Everything seems to fall right into your lap. Someone calls you. You take a wrong turn and end up in a place you have never been before. Doors open that were slammed shut in your face before.

Incidents like this don't happen while you march down the aisle to the musical interlude. They only happen as you strut down the aisle to the wedding march. (I can really go places with this analogy!)

The majority of the hindrances we face on the way to doing great things in life are the excuses we make. Excuses are the building blocks for your comfort zone.

I can't do that because...

... My right eye fell out of the socket and the doctor has to reattach it.

... My right hand shriveled up! I surely can't write that book with my left hand.

... My dog ate my invention, ran away, another inventor found him, the dog vomited the invention and the other guy made millions from my invention.

... Steven King stole my idea!

Does any of this sound silly to you? Well, it should. You see, we make up really off-the-wall excuses so we won't have to excel! We are afraid to become the success we are destined to be.

GET OUT OF YOUR OWN WAY!

If you are here for some Body, here for some Thing, and here to do great things, you need to **get out of your own way and stop making these inane excuses!**

All the excuses you make hinder progress. All excuses have a root cause.

Now, I know I gave some stupid excuses before. Let's look at some real excuses and get to the root cause of why you can't, couldn't, or shouldn't do something.

I can't do that because...

- *I tried that before and failed... Miserably.*

- *No one will ever want to hear what I have to say about that subject.*
- *I don't have the money for that. I have to buy groceries or send Little Jimmy to bugle lessons.*
- *Our family has never been successful in business. Aunt Bert and Uncle Ernie tried to go into business with Cousin Kermit and lost all of their money.*

OK, let's look at these four true-to-life excuses many people make every day.

1. **Past Miserable Failure. Y**ou may have tried the same thing before. But, did you take into consideration the people you dealt with, the economy, or your previous mindset? You may have observed folks attempting the same or similar ventures. Were they walking the right path to get to the place they attempted to reach?

   You may have dealt with people who lost their jobs or were as skeptical as you. Or, you may have told yourself every step of the way that you would fail.

   Get Out of Your OWN Way and Get Over This Excuse!

   Change your mind-set to success. Speak positive words over what you want to do. Remember: words are powerful. They can build; they can also destroy. Change the words you speak about your past successes or failures. Match those words to what you want to see accomplished in your life now.

2. **Nobody ever listened to me before; why will they listen now?** OK, so, the last book you wrote didn't sell very well. Did you ever stop to think that maybe you didn't take it to the right reading audience? Or, maybe it wasn't edited properly?

Don't give up! You've got something to say; SAY IT! If you know a little bit about anything, you can become a subject matter expert. Research. Study. Learn to write and speak about your subject.

Let me let you in on a little secret: I had to ***get out of my own way*** before I was able to write this book. I convinced my inner self that this book and the others that follow will help others. Now, it helps that I am a minister and always and forever a Drill Sergeant. More importantly, it helps that I am able to write what I know. Because I have been through it, I can help others understand the things they need to step around or avoid so they can move forward in their purpose in life.

NOTE: Let me just make an observation here: *Failure is comfortable.* Have you noticed that every time you come close to succeeding at something you really want to succeed in, you somehow sabotage all of your efforts? This is because you are afraid to succeed. *Failure is your comfort zone.* Your primary fear is stepping out of your comfort zone and success taking you to a place you really want to be. Your secondary fear is you won't know how to deal with success once you arrive. Just a thought. I personally had to deal with this. OK, back to excuses.

3. **I don't have the money for such a venture. What if I run out of money?** Unless you make needed changes in your life (**GET OUT OF YOUR OWN WAY!**) you will never have enough money to do what you really want to do. Period. Something will always come up: an unexpected bill, a chipped tooth, a pregnant pet with complications, a flat tire and a flat spare. Always. Every time you decide to do something positive about your present situation - invest in yourself by taking a marketing class or speaking or whatever - something comes up.

   Do something about the situation! Stand firm. Decide that, no matter what comes up, you will attend the seminar or training! Get a jar and start filling it with loose change and $1 bills. Sell some of the "stuff" around your house that you haven't used for years.

   Rearrange your finances to accommodate what you need to do. These opportunities that you continually make excuses about are just what you need to move forward in your purpose.

   The Drill Sergeant of Life says: Remember Life-tip #2 – S.T.E.P. into your purpose. **SEARCH; TARGET; ENGAGE; PROCEED. GET OVER YOURSELF AND YOUR SITUATION!** Search out your purpose; **T**arget it just as you would on a rifle range; **E**ngage your target - shoot it right between the eyes so that it is yours; and, **Proceed** toward the success you desire to achieve. Don't let life get in the way! **Don't let yourself get in the way!** Make life stand up and take notice. Strut down the aisle to the tune of the Wedding March of Life and not the musical interlude! Change the dynamics in your world!

4. **My family has never had their own business. No one in my family has ever gone to college. I came from the wrong side of the tracks.** Every family has an Aunt Bert, Uncle Ernie and Cousin Kermit. These three are always up to something. They want to make life better for their family but, in the end, lose their investment. They make it hard for the remainder of the family to go forward and do something worthwhile in the business realm.

You are not Aunt Bert, Uncle Ernie, or Cousin Kermit! You are smart and intelligent! You see scammers approaching 20 miles away! You know the scammer's lies and tricks. You know how they bamboozled and fooled many of your family members. They can't fool you!

You won't lose all of your money. You have prepared for this season in your life for a very long time. You know what you want to do. You know the type people you need around you. You know the type people that need to stay away. So, what's the problem?

The Drill Sergeant says: *Get Out of Your Own Way and Get Moving!*

There is nothing to fear but fear itself! You have no fear in your heart! You can do this! Everything is lined up in your favor. **You are here to do great things** and you are doing it! You were born for such a time as this. What if David had not fought Goliath? **Go fight your Goliath!**

So, how do you feel?

We have cleared up the paradoxes in your life. You are well on your way to experiencing being the Bride or Groom! Nothing can stop you because you have taken definitive actions toward what you want in life.

We have successfully blasted the root cause of why you think you can't do something. We blasted every excuse. You have discovered the underlying problems behind these excuses.

Nine times out of 10, excuses come as a result of either previous failure, discouragement from an outside source, or both. Many times, we train our brains to shut down. This act sends a signal to our subconscious that we can't do whatever is before us.

Step forward when this happens with a positive word to self,

I AM HERE FOR GREAT THINGS!

I CAN DO GREAT THINGS!

I WILL NOT FAIL!

Come on! You can do this! It may sound and seem silly, but this stuff works!

Drill Sergeant of Life-Tip #3 – Dig Up and Destroy the Root of Your Excuses!

Action Steps

- All paradoxes in my life are removed. I move forward purposefully *toward* my purpose and experience success as never before.
- Failure is comfortable; success is uncomfortable. I come out of my comfort zone and succeed at my purpose.
- Greatness is a mindset. I switch my mind frequency until I find the one I need to be in tune with: The Greatness Frequency.
- I am on track to the successes in front of me because I have learned from my previous non-successes.
- All excuses have a root cause. I dig up the root and destroy it! All my excuses shrivel up and die!

Clarity Affirmation #3

I AM HERE TO DO GREAT THINGS!

There is something on the inside of me that is excited to come out. I have trained and am in training for that some Thing to come out and present itself to the world at large. There is untapped greatness within me. I am determined to let that greatness out.

THIS IS MY SEASON!

5 BORN FOR MUCH MORE!

Look at yourself in the mirror. Really look at yourself, perhaps for the first time.

What do you see? Who do you see?

Do you have a distorted view of you and who you are supposed to be? Do you see someone who doesn't amount to much right now? Someone who will probably never amount to much?

The Drill Sergeant of Life says: *GET OVER YOURSELF AND WHAT OTHERS HAVE TOLD YOU ABOUT YOURSELF!*

Examine the motives of others in your life and look at yourself through the eyes of God. Contrary to popular belief, God does **NOT** make mistakes. Alter your views of self.

Consider changing the folks you associate with! Consider who you receive so-called "sound" advice from concerning who you really are.

I am harping about changing your view of yourself. It is something you need to consider and achieve. You see, you are your own worst critic. You are harder on yourself than you could ever be on anyone else.

You see yourself as small when others think you are a giant.

You see yourself as the least of all when, in fact, you are the greatest!

You see yourself as always the Bridesmaid and never the Bride; always the Groomsman and never the Groom. Most everyone else sees the exact opposite!

Come on, now, we are half-way there: **GET OUT OF YOUR OWN WAY AND GET WHAT YOU WANT OUT OF LIFE!**

Don't forget; you are here FOR some Body! You are here FOR some Thing! You are here TO DO great things!

Well, guess what? We have come to another tier in your learning: **You were born to be, to do, and to have more.**

SO MUCH MORE!

Your mind cannot comprehend your true potential! Your full potential is far greater than anything you could ever think for yourself.

You were created to get out there and be more than you ever thought you could be. You were brought here to the earth to do more than you ever hoped you could do in your lifetime. You were intended to have and achieve more success in your lifetime; success that will expand past you into multiple generations!

You are the Bomb!

You are Exceptional!

You are Unique!

And, you're pretty darn cute, too!

Stop it with the self put-downs!

Stop allowing others to belittle you just because they want you to do what *they* want you to do. Believe it or not, "Doormat" is not in either of the definitions for "Friend," "Co-worker," "Employee," or "Parent."

Out of the billions of people on this earth, you were created with a unique DNA. Your DNA, biological and psychological makeup consists of everything you need to excel at your purpose in doing what you were created to do.

You weren't born to do the same thing Aunt Bert was born to do. You may look like Uncle Ernie but your character is different. And as for Cousin Kermit, well....

You are strong. You are a leader. ***You are a SOLDIER in the Army of Life!***

You have more potential in the pinky toe of your left foot than your ancestors had in their entire bodies.

But, you first need to **GET OUT OF YOUR OWN WAY AND CHANGE YOUR WAY OF THINKING**.

Daily, look in the mirror of life and *see* that you are exceptional, courageous, the bomb, and more. S*ee* that you *can* make a complete turnaround and be, do and have more in your lifetime.

OK, let's look at Michael Jackson again.

NOTE: If you couldn't tell, I really liked MJ; a lot. We were the same age. He was sort of my hero growing up. He was a role model so to speak because he looked like me. You may have someone in your life who affected you in the same way.

Michael Jackson was known as the King of Pop. Do you think his parents, Joseph and Katherine, saw just a mediocre little brown-skinned boy who could sing a couple songs and maybe make a couple dollars on the side? Probably not!

If you consider the Jackson family dynamics you will see that his parents obviously saw a very distinguishable light in each of their children. The light they saw was far brighter than any others they had previously seen.

They (mostly Joseph by all reports) took their children on a journey allowing them to soar to the top of the music industry. Although Michael is now gone, consider the youngest member of the original family, Janet.

Janet Jackson is a phenomenon. In my opinion, she is the most versatile of the entire Jackson clan. I remember her debut as little Penny on **Good Times**. Even then, she stole the show from her older co-stars. She has set the world on its ear with the songs, choreography and movies she presents to the world.

So again, I ask, when you look in the mirror,

What and who do you see?

Do you see a corporate CEO or COO? Do you see a Broadway lead actor? Do you see yourself taking a call from Donald Trump to participate in a Real Estate deal?

Do you think this is farfetched? Why? It happens every day to other folks! Why not to you?

Can you see these things happening in your life? Until you **GET OUT OF YOUR OWN WAY AND CHANGE YOUR PERSONAL VIEW OF YOU**, you won't *see* any of these things happening to you.

Imagine, in your mind's eye, that you are being, doing, and having more in life. Now, look, I am not advocating materialism even though by stretching yourself, you will increase in more ways than you ever imagined!

What I am saying, though, is you need to change your self-image, your perspective of self. You need to reach for those things you really and truly want in life.

Before you were conceived in your mother's womb, the loving Almighty God invested much time, effort, and energy in you. He placed within you everything you needed to be successful in life.

He did not include mechanisms within your psyche causing you to want, desire, or hope for failure more than success; that would have been counterproductive! Doing that would have set you up for failure before you even came out of the starting gate.

Let's look back at Aunt Bert, Uncle Ernie and Cousin Kermit. Each of them started out just like you. Each of them was created by God the Creator. He saw the potential in each of them. They were all created for greatness. They could also make choices in their lives.

What if their choices had been different? What if their self-image had lined up with success rather than what had previously happened in the family? The entire family dynamic could have been different.

Instead of someone coming along and swindling Cousin Kermit and the others out of their money with some harebrained scheme that would never work, they could have become the next Rockefellers or Vanderbilt's!

Remember **C.R.A.P.P.P.P.Y.**, **S.N.A.P.P.P.Y.**, and **H.A.P.P.P.P.P.Y.Y.** from Chapter 2? Well, each of us has the potential to go from CRAPPPPPY to HAPPPPPYY: it's a choice.

You will not experience the positive side of being, doing, and having more in your life while living a CRAPPPPPY existence. Once you leave CRAPPPPPY-ville, pass through SNAPPY-burg, you eventually enter HAPPPPPYY-opolus.

In HAPPPPPPYY-opolus, you find yourself being, doing, and having more of the success you desire to experience. At the same time, you acquire a more abundant life.

Now, let's deal with this. You have always served as the Bridesmaid/Groomsman. You have never had the pleasure or opportunity of being the Bride/Groom. Every time you attempt to step out or away from the Wedding Party of Personal Mediocrity, someone comes along and makes one of the following comments:

(1) You can't go; I need you!
(2) You belong here; we need you!
(3) You'll never make it without us; you need us and we need you.

> *(4) You know you'll miss doing what you have been doing. Why don't you stay a little while longer?*
>
> (5) **Please don't go! I'm begging you to stay! I will make it better! I promise!**

Now, be honest. Haven't you heard these same comments and promises before? They usually come right after you decide you've finally had enough; right after you decide to step out so you can be, do and have more.

I know I have.

Every time an opportunity for promotion or advancement, a better opportunity outside of my current job or position came along, or I talked about leaving, suddenly (miracle of miracles!) something "better" opened up in the place I currently served. This caused a blind, a false improvement, to pop up.

This blind caused me to temporarily feel better about being there. Usually, though, after I consented to stay, things went back to normal. Shortly thereafter, I became restless and ready to move again.

This reoccurred more often than I care to remember. You see, I allowed it to happen until I realized I lived in CRAPPPPPY-ville. I Couldn't Really Achieve my Potential because I kept allowing others to Punish, Penalize, Persecute or Put me down.

My main point; **I allowed this to happen**!

I needed to **GET OUT OF MY OWN WAY** so I could **GET WHAT I WANTED OUT OF LIFE AND REALLY ENJOY MYSELF!**

Let me interject a true story here as an example. You see, in Romans 8:28, the Bible says,

And we know that all things work together for good to them that love God, to them who are the called according to His purpose.

I needed a break from the wedding party I currently served in. God, through a situation with my Dad, made that break possible.

I was given the opportunity to get away from my current position in the bridal party. During that season, I looked at me deeply, very deeply; no one else; only me. I considered all I had done in life and where I currently stood.

I glanced in the mirror of my life. What I saw was not pretty. As a matter of fact, it was downright ugly, sad and pathetic...

I saw that, although I had been a big help to the bridal party I was currently serving in, I could have made a bigger splash as the Bride.

I saw that, not only had I let Almighty God, my husband and children down, I let myself down. I had forgotten my true purpose in life. I had forgotten how to be a SOLDIER!

I had forgotten that I was here <u>for</u> some Body, <u>for</u> some Thing, and <u>to do</u> Great Things.

You see, by this season of my life, I had already started (and prematurely ended) several businesses and ministries that could have been very successful had I kept running with them. I had experienced phenomenal success with a marketing company and climbed their ranks very quickly.

Life set in causing me to lose focus. Two beloved family members passed away within three months of each other: my stepmother and my father-in-law. After their deaths, I lost my momentum, zeal, and courage and stopped running with my purpose.

It was a long time before I considered coming out of the funk that had set in over a number of years. Life (or so I thought) had beaten up on me very badly. It wasn't life; it was me! I needed to **Get Out Of My Own Way!**

By the time my Dad called requesting that I come to NY to help him during a series of several eye surgeries, status quo was more than enough for me. I didn't want to start anything for fear that I would experience failure... again.

Many folks willingly supported my theory for their benefit. The Wedding Party attempted to lure me back into its clutches to serve as usual.

After glancing into the mirror of my life and seeing how ugly, sad, and pathetic I appeared, something kicked in within my psyche.

I stopped listening to the sincere and insincere pleadings of others. They attempted to make me feel better about staying with them because they **needed** me. I deliberately stepped back and had a good talk with **Beatrice**.

Girl, you need to get over yourself, get out of your own way so that you can get what YOU want out of life! It's not up to other folks! God has given YOU everything YOU need to go forth and do what YOU are supposed to be doing! GET BUSY!!

Once I finally put my foot down (after my hiatus in NY, it was a very short time!) I got S.N.A.P.P.P.Y.:

Immediately, I **S**tarted **N**ow **A**chieving my **P**otential by **P**romoting and **P**ushing myself.

I met some people completely out of my regular sphere of influence; I began networking. I had always been a little leery of networking and, I will admit, hated doing it! But, the folks I met lit a four-foot fire under my 5'10" behind! I have been running ever since I met them.

They showed me that I *can* do what needs to be done to get my family and me to where we need to be. They also reminded me that if I **ask**, I shall receive; if I **seek**, I shall find; if I **knock**, the door shall be opened unto me (Matthew 7:7.)

I began to view myself differently. I looked at my past successes and made a decision:

If I did it before, surely I can do it again!

I changed my self-speak. Just like Romans 4:17, I called those things that weren't, **YET**, as though they were already evident in my life.

Now, I didn't want the particular Groom of where I had
served (remember, this applies to every aspect of your
life!) I wanted my own. The only way I would find my
Groom and he find me was to S.T.E.P. into my purpose.

I had to step down and away from the Bridal Party of
Personal Mediocrity. You see, as part of this bridal party,
I didn't have any real responsibility; all I had to do was
show up. That's all!

Show up. Smile. March down the aisle. Shed a few tears
at the appropriate time. Amen at the "I Dos." March back
down the aisle. Go to the reception. And, hope, **HOPE** to
catch the bridal bouquet. (For the Groomsmen, you hoped
to catch the garter, didn't you?)

I never caught the bouquet! I never got to go on the
honeymoon!

All I did was smile and fake it because I really didn't
want or need to be there. Can you relate?

I really needed to *GET OUT OF BEATRICE'S WAY!*

For many years, I believed the sad stories the various
Brides or Grooms told me. I was their willing dupe.

*We **need** you!*

*You **can't** leave!*

*You'll **miss** us!*

Had I used common sense, I would have realized the
truth: as I stepped out, another quickly replaced me!

The Drill Sergeant of Life says: *GET OUT OF YOUR OWN WAY!!!*

You are here for so much more. You are incredible! But, you need to S.T.E.P.!

SEARCH out your purpose. This is critical. If you encounter a false purpose, one that fits but is not for you, you could end up in the Bridal Party of Personal Mediocrity and get stuck there again.

Once you find your true purpose, put a **TARGET** on it. Remember the old bulls-eye with crosshairs at center mass? You need to *see* your purpose so you can put the TARGET on it. Time is of the essence.

There was an older gentleman in the Bible named Abram. When he was 99 years old, God came to him and told him that he and his 89 year-old wife, Sarai, were going to have a son by natural birth. I know: 89 and 99 years of age? Riiiiiightttttttttt!

But, God changed Abram's and Sarai's names to Abraham (Father of many nations) and Sarah (Princess.) In doing so, He caused them to obtain a different view of themselves. Before, Abram had not borne any children and Sarai was barren.

God indicated in His covenant with Abraham that He had changed the dynamic in his life. **You** need to change the dynamic in your life. You need to see your new purpose and personality. Just as Abraham did, you need to **TARGET** your purpose by calling it as though it already exists in your life.

After you acquire the TARGET, **ENGAGE** it. Don't allow it to get out of your sight! The next time, the acquisition of the TARGET may not be as easy.

After you ENGAGE the TARGET, **PROCEED.** In other words, move forward.

Once you make the final decision to S.T.E.P. out of the Wedding Party of Personal Mediocrity, things will happen for you. Some of the things are good. Annnndddd... some of the things will _**appear**_ to be bad.

Good Things

1. Previously closed doors now open wide for you.
2. You have new encounters. You encounter new opportunities of advancement and success.
3. New associations take you further into your purpose.
4. You experience more positive events in your life.
5. You _**see**_ yourself as more of the success you want to be.
6. You _**do**_ more things creating even greater success and HAPPPPPYY-ness in your life.
7. You experience _**more**_ abundance in every aspect of your life. Physical, mental, spiritual, and financial.

Because you have decided to S.T.E.P. away from mediocrity and into your true purpose in life, these and other good things occur in your life. **And it feels wonderful!**

When you look back, you feel sad but good about everything you endured to get to where you are now.

Now, don't get discouraged when you also stumble upon some *seemingly* bad events as you S.T.E.P. forward into your purpose.

Seemingly Bad Things

1. Life goes on. The wedding party moves forward leaving you behind. After all, you are no longer with them. You decide to not be a Bridesmaid/ Groomsman anymore. You decide to become the Bride/Groom.
2. You lose some long-time attachments as you move forward into your true purpose. Don't allow the loss to slow you down. Even though you lose some relationships, you gain even more. Your previous relationships served their purpose. Those relationships pushed you out and up toward your ultimate purpose. Take the time to get over these previous attachments (I know it hurts and may even take a minute, but you need to do it!)
3. Faces change. Very few faces remain with you all the days of your life. Accept this and move on. Just as the seasons on the earth change from spring, to summer, to fall, to winter, the seasons in our lives change as well. Make conscience decisions to move on so you can be, do, and have more. In doing this, you bless God for having equipped you with this purpose. Because you are finally fulfilling your purpose, you also bless yourself and your family. Embrace the new attachments appearing in your life for all they are worth. Observe the realness and the deeper meanings behind the activation of these attachments.

You are now the Bride/Groom: you have a bridal party to attend to!

You learned a lot from your time as a Bridesmaid/Groomsman. Put to good use everything you learned. Remember how you felt when you were in that lowly position? Well, it's your turn to **not** make someone else feel the same way.

What an incredible journey for you in your new role on top of the wedding cake! Look at all the layers below you! WOW! Take a moment to compose yourself! You finally made it to the top!

Now that you have STEPped into your purpose and discovered that you were born to *be, do, and have more*, take the opportunity to help others be, do, and have more in their lives.

I am excited for you! You are incredible!

Now comes the hard part: Have faith and believe in yourself.

Know in your heart that Almighty God knew what He was doing when He created you. His purpose in creating you was for you to become who you are right now. You can *be, do, and have more* than you could ever imagine! Your brain can't wrap itself around all that is going on in your life.

You have a whole new bridal party rooting for you!

When you look in the mirror of life now, can you **see** yourself transformed into the Bride/Groom, looking and feeling like a million bucks?

Can you **see** yourself seated at the head of **your** corporate boardroom table giving direction?

Can you **see** yourself on the Broadway stage as the lead and no longer in the supporting role?

Can you **see** yourself on the concert stage, a lead singer singing, as Joe Sabah says, *the song you were meant to sing?*

I Can!

This is your time!

Now is your season!

You were **NOT** created to always struggle through life and only have just enough to get by. You were created to *be, do, and have more*! It is your time to do just that!

GET OUT OF YOUR OWN WAY SO YOU CAN BE, DO, AND HAVE MORE!

Some Body is waiting for you to *be, do, and have more*. She or he *needs* to see you succeed so they can experience that same hope within. That hope alone will catapult them to the next level in life.

Some Thing is waiting for you to grab it and make it do what it is supposed to do. In turn, some Body is waiting for you to grab this "thing" because they need it... **NOW!**

You can't afford to wait any longer. You have waited long enough. You have been held captive by the

Please don't go's!

and the,

I can't live without yous!

far too long!

It is your turn!

S.T.E.P. out of the Bridal Party of Personal Mediocrity and into the *Wedding Gala of Success.* You were created to participate in this Gala. You won't regret your move!

Great things await you. These great things need you so they can be accomplished.

You are exceptional! You were born to do great things in your life!

It's **NOT** too late! As a matter of fact, this season is right on time!

You spent all this time in preparation for a reason: when you hit the doors of the universe, everyone knows you have arrived. They quickly step back and make way for you! They pay attention to what you say and do because they have awaited your arrival with great expectancy. They are so glad you finally arrived!

As you begin your journey, you become strengthened in your abilities. Your successes happen just like clockwork.

Not only do your bank accounts grow enabling you to have more, you become and do more and more as you grow more skilled in fulfilling your purposes on the earth.

Remember who you are! Remember what you look like! You can't fail; it's not in your destiny. Because you were created for success, you only succeed!

You **can be, do, and have more** of everything you have ever hoped, dreamed or desired.

The Drill Sergeant says...*GET OVER YOURSELF, GET OUT OF YOUR OWN WAY AND GET WHAT YOU WANT OUT OF LIFE!*

I believe in you! Believe in yourself!

There is some "Thing" you are here on the earth for. This "Thing" can only come through you.

Your personal spin can cause this "Thing" to be special, unique. Yes, many others before you have produced similar things. But *this* "Thing" only comes through you.

It has been carefully planned and thought out. Almighty God determined it in His Heart. He will bring it to pass through you if you will allow Him.

Don't judge your future by what happened in the past. You are not your past! You look at yourself differently. So...

GET OUT OF YOUR OWN WAY AND GO AND BE, DO, AND HAVE MORE!

Be more courageous than ever before.

Do more of what you know and were called to do.

Have more successes.

The time is yours. Your dreams, hopes, and desires are not dead. **Neither are you!**

GO AND GET WHAT YOU WANT OUT OF LIFE!

Drill Sergeant of Life-Tip #4 – Have Faith And Believe In Yourself!

Action Steps

- ✓ Change your view of you. You are not what others say you are. See yourself differently and you will be different.
- ✓ Call those things that aren't as though they are. Speak about the things you want as though already evident in your life.
- ✓ Remember all you have learned. Now that you are the Bride/Groom, treat others the way you want to be treated.
- ✓ You are not your ancestor. You are exceptional. You are wonderful! You are free to pursue your dream, your destiny. Be the "you" you were created to be.
- ✓ Picture the "you" you want to be. In order for you to have it, you must see it first. Take time to meditate on what you want, get it in your mind, and then run with it. You CAN have it!

Clarity Affirmation #4

I AM HERE TO BE, DO, AND HAVE MORE!

I am here to be courageous and to show more courage than I ever have before. I am courageous!

I am here to do more of what I know and what I was called to do!

I am here to have more successes than I have ever experienced in my life!

6 GROWING UP AND GROWING OUT

Can we talk about the Bible for a bit? This Book of Books is very precious to me.

Some folks say the Bible is a fable. Others say it has good advice but you can't take it literally.

Well, I take the Bible literally and, in my opinion, it is not a fable. It is the Word of God or God's love letter to me. It is your choice to see it in the way you want to see it. But, as for me...

In this chapter, we will discuss one particular verse of scripture from the Bible. The Book of I Corinthians contains a chapter folks in Christian circles refer to as the "Love" chapter.

In it, the writer, Apostle Paul, writes about love. He wrote this book in the New Testament after converting to Christianity. The chapter gives an accurate and active definition of love.

The verse I want to concentrate on is I Corinthians 13:11. It says:

When I was a child, I spake as a child, I understood as a child, I thought as a child; but when I became a man, I put away childish things.

Hmmmm. Interesting, isn't it?

Apostle Paul wrote in AD 56 or so that, as he grew older, things in his life changed. These changes caused his perspective to take on a different light. These changes also caused him to remove certain things from his life.

He needed to remove these things so he could grow up in the purpose for which he was called. He needed to grow outward into the fulfillment of his true purpose.

Next to Jesus Christ, Apostle Paul is probably one of the most interesting characters in the Bible. Paul wrote from his heart. He also operated from his heart in everything he did, especially before his conversion to Christianity.

Now, even though the things he did prior to his conversion were contrary to God's true purpose for his life, Paul did things from his heart, with all his heart and with all his might! That's the way we are supposed to operate in every aspect of our lives.

Before his conversion, Apostle Paul hated Christians - their culture, religion, and faith. He dramatically changed after his conversion experience. He came to know and understand true love. He discovered the love God had for him even as he persecuted God's people.

The reason I want to discuss verse 11 is to show you the growing up or maturation process we all eventually go through in our lives. When we do, the process enables us to see things in a different light.

Paul shared that when he was a child, he spoke like a child spoke, understood things in the same way a child understood things, and thought in ways only children thought.

Now that's saying something!

If you are around children at all, you realize the way children see things are abstract from the way adults see the same or similar things. Children speak a different language. They see things adults don't see. They think differently.

When I was a child, I saw gorillas and elephants in the clouds very easily. Now, though, as an adult, it's hard for me to conceptualize the clouds, cumulus nimbus or whatever they are, as being anything but what they are: clouds.

We lose something when we lose the ability to see some things, not all things, the way children see them. Yes, we do! Anyway...

But let's break this verse down a little...

I spake as a child...

Take a moment and think back as far as you can to when you were a child. Now, many of us can't remember the first words we spoke or the first sentence we strung together.

We probably said such things as:

Mama, Dadda, Doggie, Mine,

...and other one or two syllable words. These words were easy and simply rolled off our tongues.

As we grew older and became toddlers, we strung words together to form easy phrases like,

Hungry, Mama!

Want down!

or, ***Want go out!***

These phrases served our purposes well until we were able to string together more words to form more complex sentences.

I don't want to!

You're mean; I'm telling!

I don't want peas! I don't like them. They're yucky!

By this time, we were more than likely ready for preschool or kindergarten. Upon beginning our primary education, we wrote and talked better than earlier in our lives. We formed even more complex sentences framing the foundation of our understanding and thoughts.

But, we did all this as children. Many of the sentences we spoke then were long forgotten as we entered our secondary years of education in Junior, Middle or High School.

By this time, we formed yet more complex thoughts. We understood literary prose and scientific calculations that, unless we were child geniuses, we could not firmly grasp with our childish minds.

Apostle Paul shared that when he became a man, he stopped talking like a child. He was able to understand the words he spoke in a way he never understood as a child.

He probably found that some of the words he used were unintentionally rude, crude, or socially unacceptable. His words offended some people in ways they did not when he was a child.

He spoke as a child, he understood as a child, he thought as a child. As we grow older, life forces us to speak, understand and think differently. Whereas it's ok to say certain things as a child, we find these same things are politically and socially incorrect when we become adults.

When Apostle Paul became a man, he put away childish things.

What sorts of things? you might wonder. Things such as attitudes, preconceived notions, and thought patterns come to mind. But, let's look at this verse in two ways: literally and spiritually.

In the literal sense, a person is born, goes from infancy through childhood, through adolescence to adulthood. This is according to the seasons of life as we know it. This is how God the Creator determined we would reach the level of maturity He designed for us.

As children, we do things differently than we do as adults.

Duh! right?

But, consider this... How many people do you know who, biologically and physically are adults, yet, mentally and emotionally, are still children? Hello!

You know the ones I'm talking about. You've been around them for so long, you may not recognize them.

These are the folks in your sphere who are *always* needy. They can't seem to put two coherent thoughts together to come to a solid conclusion concerning the instability in their lives. They always look for someone else to answer questions concerning their lives; questions they should be answering themselves.

These precious ones, whom we love dearly, continually pull on us to help them. But, they won't help themselves!

We enable them because we feel sorry for them. They don't have a clue how to get themselves together. Friend, let me just say this:

The Drill Sergeant of Life says: *Get Over Yourself And Tell Your Friend To Get Over Him Or Herself!*

I am not here to enable you. As a matter of fact, **I will not enable you!** I will encourage you, though.

I encourage you to speak plainly, with love, to your friend about getting his or her life together. If not, 10, 15, 20 years from now, this person will still go through the same circumstances he or she faces right now. He or she will be no closer to where he or she needs to be in life.

And, their *purpose*? Forget about it! Why should he or she worry about purpose while being surrounded by folks who baby them every step of the way?

To be honest, **you** need to **GET OVER YOURSELF** more than your friend. You let the *power of need* keep you from saying what needs to be said to this person. That inaction causes more, much more harm than good.

118

You see, even though this person's body has matured quite nicely, the mind is still stuck in childhood.

The person who has not matured in his or her mind continually speaks, understands, and thinks in the same way a child does.

I'm grown; I don't have to listen to you!

How dare you speak to me that way! Do you know who I am ?!?!?!

You're going to pay for that! I will get you back! Just watch!

These childish thoughts are indicative of the speaker's need to get over him or herself. These thoughts and comments demonstrate the person's lack of maturity. The person who speaks like this is caught up in their own thoughts and understanding. He or she misses out on the great teaching moments going on in their situation.

The Drill Sergeant of Life says: *You REALLY Need To Get Over Yourself!*

There is always more to learn than what meets the eye.

As you continue to ponder the powerful message in this verse of scripture, let's switch to the spiritual ramifications behind it.

While studying to become a Bible scholar, Paul got on the wrong track concerning faith, religion and, especially, Christianity. He collaborated with groups of scholars who believed and taught that Christianity was wrong.

Listening to these folks in his immaturity, he persecuted all Christians: threw some in jail, whipped others, assisted in stoning others. (And you say he wrote the chapter on **love**? Oh, boy!)

Paul was very immature in the way he received God's Word. Subsequently, by doing what he did with what he received, he illustrated that he didn't fully understand what he was taught.

His thought processes were clouded by the way he was taught and how he understood what he was taught. The people surrounding Paul were instrumental in helping him act and think in the way he did.

Then, one day, he had an encounter with the One Whom he had persecuted above all others: Jesus Christ.

But when I became a man, I put away childish things.

In the Jewish culture, boys are counted as men at the age of 13. This age is considered to be the age of accountability, when Jewish males are ready to make their own decisions and go forward into manhood.

Spiritually, however, the age of accountability or maturation can unfortunately come at a much later time.

In Paul's case, it came when he encountered Jesus on the road to Damascus. Not only was Paul converted and physically blinded, he received a deeper revelation of Jesus and His plan for mankind.

Don't you think it interesting that such drastic measures had to be taken with this Bible scholar? These measures caused Paul to understand the truth about the people he frequently persecuted. He was *blinded* before he could **see** the truth!

This same phenomenon happens to us in this day and age. Most of the time, we cannot see the obstacles in our lives hindering us from moving forward in the purpose we were created for.

Just a little something to consider.

Paul, on the other hand, discovered that Jesus, a Jew, gave up his life to save all mankind from the flood of sin it drowned in. Once Paul understood this, straight from the mouth of Christ, as it were, he thought, understood, and spoke differently about Christianity.

Paul saw the relevance of Christianity. He understood how it pertained to him. This new understanding and new way of thought revolutionized Paul's life. It caused him to go forth and preach the true Gospel of Jesus Christ.

Now, please understand: this is not written to persuade you to convert to Christianity. The Apostle Paul is an excellent example of someone who needed to **GET OVER HIMSELF AND GET OUT OF HIS OWN WAY**.

He persecuted folks just because he could. He arrested Christian men, women, and children just because they were Christians. He voluntarily held the coats of those who stoned Evangelist Stephen to death. Paul needed to put away childish things so he could be the man God had called him to be.

Because our speech, understanding and thoughts are immature or childish, there are many ways in which we persecute others or allow others to persecute us

We need to **grow up and get over ourselves.** Immaturity often causes our purpose to be delayed, diminished or defeated.

Have you ever wondered why your true purpose has not appeared in your life yet? Well, perhaps you are immature and can't handle your purpose yet. You may be at a stage in life in which immaturity has caused your purpose to be delayed.

When your growth is stunted, your purpose diminishes. The effectiveness of your purpose is diminished because of your actions or inactions. You defeat your purpose by being immature and unable to handle the responsibilities of your purpose.

You need to be able to command the full scope of your purpose. Why do you think so many people fail at what they should be very good at? Because the majority of them are too immature to carry out the full responsibility of their purpose.

Now, immaturity shows up in many different ways. For the purpose of discussing the Bridesmaid Syndrome, immaturity shows up in the person who is always held back by others. This person is never ready to step forward in their destiny.

Look around yourself. Have you noticed the other Bridesmaids moving on and becoming Brides while you still serve as a Bridesmaid? Have you become the elder over the next generation of Groomsmen? If this is the case, **Get Over Yourself, Get Out of Your Own Way, And Step Up Your Game!**

In order to alleviate the *always* and *never* aspects of the Bridesmaid Syndrome, you need to S.T.E.P. forward in maturity. It's up to **you** to change the dynamic you have operated under for so long.

The gifts and calling God the Creator gave to us are for our use and profit the entire time we are on the Earth. Our main purpose, the purpose that never changes, is to fulfill the gifts and callings on our lives. These gifts and callings are installed within us for the benefit of being a blessing to Almighty God and to all of mankind.

When we remain immature, our purpose and the gifts and calling remain unused and unfulfilled. What a shame and a waste!

We need to ***get over ourselves and grow up*** so we can be the productive people we were created to be. And we were all created to be productive!

Come on, let's reaffirm:

- **I AM HERE <u>FOR</u> SOME BODY!**
- **I AM HERE <u>FOR</u> SOME THING!**
- **I AM HERE <u>TO DO</u> GREAT THINGS!**
- **I AM HERE <u>TO BE, DO, AND HAVE</u> SO MUCH MORE!**
- **I HAVE A <u>S.E.T.</u> PURPOSE!**

As we close this chapter, think about this: you are not here to be persecuted, mistreated or browbeaten.

If you are being persecuted and allowing these actions repeatedly, you need to **grow up and get over yourself!** It's up to you to become the person you were created to be.

Many people persecute others because they have permission to do so. By the same token, many people are persecuted because they believe what others say about them. Don't allow this to happen to you. These folks love you but not enough to stop persecuting you.

Remove yourself from this behavior!

Remove yourself from these folks who only believe in their concept of you!

You have to force yourself to **grow up and grow out** of these relationships so you can fulfill the purpose for which you were created.

Don't continue to be bullied!

Stop being bullied so Some Body can see your purpose fulfilled in you.

Stop being bullied, S.T.E.P. into your purpose and create the some "Thing" you came here to create.

The Drill Sergeant of Life says, *Great things are waiting for you!*

Take your life back! Move forward with excellence in the purpose you were created to fulfill.

Begin working with other purposeful folks. They will guide you forward with a vengeance into the thing you are more than capable of doing.

Stop prattling on like a child! Stop limiting yourself with immature thoughts. Increase your understanding of your purpose so you can run with it. Remove the Naysayers and Unbelievers from your life. After all, like Apostle Paul they are blind to what you are really here for.

The Drill Sergeant of Life says, *Get Over Yourself, Get Out Of Your Own Way, And Get On With Life! We Need You For Real!!!*

NOTE: I am so very proud of you for making it this far! I rejoice in your accomplishments and achievements. So should you!

Drill Sergeant of Life-Tip #5 – Separate Yourself From Unbelievers

Action Steps

- Don't believe everyone's thoughts about you. Their opinions are just that: opinions. Not everyone has your best interests at heart.
- Change the scenery in your life. This is a season of change. You can't keep everyone in your life. You are growing in ways they may never grow.
- Grow up and Grow out. Force yourself to grow up or mature. Cause yourself to grow out of certain environments. Repot yourself giving you more room to grow.
- Believe in you. Speak positively when others speak negatively about you. It is YOUR life, YOUR direction! If you don't speak positively about you, how will others?
- Get on TOP of the Wedding Cake of Life!

Clarity Affirmation #5

I Have a S.E.T. Purpose!

Strategic – My purpose is continually being worked out as I walk and grow in it.

Evolutionary – My purpose is always evolving from the basic to the complex as I grow into my purpose.

Tactical – My purpose is suitable for bringing about the results I desire to fulfill my destiny.

PHASE III

GET WHAT **YOU** WANT OUT OF LIFE!

7 YES, YOU CAN! YES, YOU WILL!

OK. We've covered a lot of ground.

In **Chapter One,** you discovered that you are a Soldier in the Army of Life. You enlisted into the ***Get Over Yourself Boot-Camp*** and entered Phase I of your training to **Get Over Yourself!**

In **Chapter Two**, you discovered that it really isn't about you. It's about the people you were created and sent here to impact. The common thread throughout is we absolutely need to **get over ourselves** so we can find our purpose and make the impact we were created to make.

In **Chapter Two**, you also learned how to turn your life from C.R.A.P.P.P.P.P.Y. to H.A.P.P.P.P.P.P.Y.Y.

In **Chapter Three**, you realized that you were born with a purpose. You learned how to S.T.E.P. into your purpose by **searching**, **targeting**, **engaging** and **proceeding** toward your purpose.

Some folks experience their purpose virtually falling into their laps; they are the lucky ones. The rest of us, though, have to search for our purpose as though it is hidden treasure. Once we find it, we guard it, take care of it, and nurture it so it will grow into something magnificent.

In **Chapter Four**, you S.T.E.P.ped away from *always* being the Bridesmaid and *never* the Bride. You decided (and so did I!) to **Never More** be anything other than successful at the helm of your own destiny. Although others need and rely on you, you discovered that you sometimes allowed their neediness to overpower your sense of rightness in doing what you were called and created to do.

In **Chapter Four,** you also chose to go forward and make your mark even if you have to leave some people behind. Some of these folks are well-meaning and loving and some are not so well-meaning and loving (even though they think they are!) Last but not least, you learned to put excuses in their place; out of your life.

Chapter Five helped you claim your birthright of being, doing, and having so much more than you have allowed yourself to have to this point. You learned to **get out of your own way** and be more courageous in the face of adversity. You learned to do more of your purpose and less of what others expected. Finally, you discovered how to have and create more successes in your life so you could go further and higher than ever before.

Are you excited yet?

In **Chapter Six**, you followed the life of one Apostle Paul who illustrated the importance of putting away childish things and maturing into your purpose. You saw how, although our bodies aged appropriately according to our numbered age, our minds may not mature as quickly. This means we must allow our inner workings to rise higher. We need to become mature in every aspect of our lives so our speech, thoughts and understanding match our stature in life.

And now on to Chapter Seven!

In case you haven't caught on yet, the message of this book is *GET OVER YOURSELF, GET OUT OF YOUR OWN WAY, AND GET WHAT YOU WANT OUT OF LIFE!*

You've grown quite comfortable serving as an attendant in the Wedding Party of Personal Mediocrity. You love all the familiar faces and attitudes. You love not having any responsibility other than to show up, look cute, nod, shed a tear, and smile.

Well, **the Drill Sergeant of Life says,** *that season in your life is over, Soldier! It is time to move into YOUR purpose!*

That is, if you want it to be.

I must warn you, though; if you are not willing for this transformation to take place in your life, you can read books from now until the cows come home. None of what you read will make a bit of difference!

- **YOU** need to want this!'
- **YOU** need to make forward steps!
- **YOU** need to believe in yourself as much as others believe in you!
- **YOU** need to love yourself more than you love being comfortable in mediocrity!

The onus is on you!

I will not enable you! I will encourage you. I can only take you by the hand for so long and so much. At some point, **you** need to let go of my hand and toddle on into your purpose, under your own steam.

You can do this! You will do this if you **Get Over Yourself and Get Out Of Your Own Way!** You need to move forward in the direction you know to move in so you can **Get What YOU Want Out of Life!**

Will it all be smooth sailing? **Probably not!**

There will be times you will want to quit. There will even be times in which you will quit for a minute, get your bearing and start all over again.

At times, you will look in the mirror of life and say to yourself,

I have completely lost my mind! (OK, maybe that last part was just for me!)

Others will question your motives. They will come to you spewing doubt. They won't believe you should be doing what you are doing because **THEY** don't feel right about it.

More than likely, these are the same people you served faithfully for years as a Bridesmaid or Groomsman.

You see, these folks have a vested interest in you not succeeding because of one of four reasons:

(1) They can say, *I told you so!*
(2) You can come back to them where you belong.
(3) **Your** success puts *them* in the position of being the Bridesmaid. (**NOTE:** What they fail to realize is that they were always there but were sucking the life out of you to make them the Bride. You,

being so into the "Bridesmaid" part in life, couldn't see it.)

(4) Just because...

Just because WHAT? you say.

Just because... Misery does in fact love company. They're not moving forward: **How dare you even think you can move forward!** Who do you think YOU are?!!?

Just because... They would rather see you fail - so you can tuck your tail between your legs and come back to them broken and needy – than succeed and prove them wrong.

Yes, these are your friends and loved ones!

And, *just because...* They don't want to see you succeed because you won't need them anymore. Or, you won't be a Bridesmaid anymore.

The gist of the matter, though, is this: if this person truly had a viable relationship with you, he or she would want you to move forward. Why? Because, when you move forward, you just might motivate them to do the same.

You see, people fail to realize we are actually in this thing called "life" together. We are happy and sad... Together.

I don't believe in that old maxim,

Laugh and the world laughs with you. Cry and you cry alone.

Nope, that's not true in my book.

Recent events around the world have caused all of us to cry together. Floods, tsunamis, earthquakes, tornadoes, hurricanes, mine disasters...

While viewing the heartbreaking telecasts from around the world, don't tell me your heart didn't shed a tear because of the devastation in the lives of the victims! Devastation we could all face at any given moment.

To see those little old Japanese men and women weeping with joy and sorrow: joy at being alive; sorrow because they have lost numerous loved ones in the floods that completely demolished their lives. Please!

You see, it is important to **get over yourself**, **S.T.E.P.** into your purpose and move forward in life. Just as you are here for some Body, for some Thing, and to do great Things, the Body's and Things are waiting for you to put your hand in and do what you are supposed to do.

There is someone somewhere right now crying because you haven't moved forward. They are devastated because that "Thing" you are supposed to do is created specifically for them. Skeptical, huh? Well, check this out.

Thomas Edison tried and failed hundreds of times before he invented a viable solution to light without candles. Aren't you glad he went forward in his purpose?

Wouldn't it be hard driving your car without headlights? How about flying in an airplane or traveling on a train without lights? I don't think so.

Some Body is waiting for you to do what you were created to do. They want to come out of the mediocrity and darkness they currently reside in and have lived in for so long. So, you say you need another example?

What about that annoying little piece of plastic and wires that rings at the most inopportune times? What if Alexander Graham Bell had gotten no further than two cans attached by strings? You wouldn't even be able to telegraph your folks thousands of miles away. You would still be waiting for the Pony Express, wouldn't you?

You see, we rarely consider those folks who came, left their mark on society, and went on to glory after fulfilling their purpose in life. We take for granted their contributions to our world. We are so caught up in other folks doing great things but not us. But, guess what?

YES! YOU CAN!

YES! YOU WILL!

That is if you really want to. The choice is yours. The decision is there for you to make.

The Drill Sergeant of Life says: *GET OVER YOURSELF, GET OUT OF YOUR OWN WAY, AND GET WHAT YOU WANT OUT OF LIFE!*

Look at yourself with fresh eyes.

You are an awesome creature. The things you did in the past had the potential to be superb, outstanding even. You held back because no one pushed you forward. **You never pushed yourself forward!** No one took up your cause to be excellent because you didn't take up your own cause!

You feel the need inside of yourself right now, though, don't you? Something has changed inside you. You feel different.

You have caught an impulse you never experienced before. You reach down deep inside and pull up those images of your successful self you pushed to the back of your mind. You think to yourself,

Well, maybe I can. Maybe I will.

You're not certain yet but the possibility is there.

You think about it even more now. You dust off strategies you created before and look at them with fresh eyes. HMMMMMMM!

You go to the library or search the internet for ideas and solutions to the images now flooding your mind. It seems more doable as each moment passes. You get excited!

WARNING: Just because **you** are excited does not mean **everyone** you share this with will be excited for you! Now is the time the Naysayers and Unbelievers will show their true nature!

Don't get defeated or discouraged. Now is not the time! Put up your defenses! This is *your* purpose, *your* dream! Don't let these folks beat you before you get a good jump out of the starting box!

A word of advice: **don't tell everyone what you are doing!** Not only will this keep you focused, it will also cut down on much of the negativity that is sure to come.

Look for mentors/encouragers to motivate and encourage you beyond the discouragement. Look for some folks who have taken risks and beaten the odds.

Create positive self-talk messages for yourself. These messages will defy all those Naysayers and Unbelievers and keep them at bay.

Maintain a proper perspective and push forward into your purpose.

OK. So, now you have a running start. You're doing research on-line and at the library. You meditate on action steps you need to take. You have a strong start, a consistent run, and set yourself up for a stupendous finish.

And you run.

And you run.

And you run.

You see some results but they are not what you hoped. You continue to run, optimistic, hopeful. Others who started after you *seem* to be passing you as you check out your surroundings. You begin to question yourself.

Am I doing all the right things?

Am I making the right moves?

Why am I not progressing?

You review your strategy; everything checks out. You put your nose back to the grindstone. You see a little more progress. At the same time, you also notice more late starters passing you by. You choose to ignore.

You push yourself harder. After all, you've come too far to stop or turn around. You go to the nearest farm goods store and purchase a pair of blinders.

That's the ticket! Those blinders work!

Now you have your focus back! You can't and don't want to see what everyone else is doing. It causes distractions you don't need right now. You learn something new: **F.O.C.U.S.**

You are **Fixed**

On your

Calling, and experiencing

Unusual

Success

Hah! You've got this thing beat and you know it. **HALLELUJAH!**

Your mind does a complete revamp and turn around. You stubbornly fix on your purpose, your true calling in life. You completely tune out those voices set on turning you away from your purpose. Your brow is set. You constantly, continually put your nose to the grindstone.

You train with Olympic Athletic precision and determination. You decide that whatever does not have anything to do with your calling and purpose gets placed on the back burner.

People marvel at your **F.O.C.U.S.** They have never observed such determination in you!

Pretty soon, instead of talking *about* you, they talk *to* and *with* you to see exactly **what** you are doing. You become an inspiration to many as you dig in deeper. Your habits change. They now reflect a confident, determined, new you on a mission.

Your mission: Fulfill your purpose on the earth so that Almighty God is blessed by your fruitfulness. Others become enriched and educated by your success. You and your family are prospering, profiting and profoundly blessed by *you* doing what you were created to do!

Doesn't that feel great?

You have a deeper understanding and appreciation of your innate abilities than ever before. You appreciate your achievements more. You applaud yourself for your true accomplishments. You no longer pooh-pooh your successes as flukes; you see and receive them for what they are: **SUCCESS!**

You feel great! You look great! You are a changed person. You are no longer the Bridesmaid or the Groomsman. You are the Bride! You are the Groom!

And you do this without becoming a Bridezilla or a Groomothra!

You move with charm and grace. You exude confidence, maturity, love and peace wherever you go! Joy overflows from you! Your joy continually touches the lives of those you find constantly around you.

By the way, the dynamics have changed in your sphere of influence. No longer are you viewed as Meek Martha or Just Justin. You are more relevant than ever before.

Your sphere **wants** to hear from you. They call **you** for advice rather than calling to give you (usually bad) advice. They want what you have in a good way. And you give it!

You should be really pumped right about now!

The blood coursing through your veins pushes out all the negativity and replaces it with powerful positivity and probability. You face any and all challenges with fresh resolve to get the job done. There is nothing you can't do! There is nothing you won't do to fulfill your destiny.

Come On! Proclaim it to the world!

YES, I CAN! YES, I WILL!

You know what your purpose is! **S.T.E.P.** into it! Put a name on it! Put your time and energy into it! Put your life into it!

Remember, no one makes a splash by sitting on the shore! You have to jump; jump high and with purpose and determination to make a splash that will set the world on fire!

You come out of your comfort zone. Don't stop there! Break down every barrier that presents its ugly head so there are no more comfort zones in your way.

As a matter of fact, gain a new perspective: you thrive only in the uncomfortable! If it is the edge of the seat, that's where you belong! If it is hanging by a horrific thread, this is the place you need to be!

Many of the world's wealthiest and most elite people and businesses were built by seat-of-the-pants experiences. These people willfully and willingly risked practically everything to experience successes few will ever achieve behind them.

You have the potential to do the very same. Step by step, minute by minute, you create the life you desire. But, you have to get out of the way.

You have to **GET OVER YOURSELF, GET OUT OF YOUR OWN WAY AND BECOME THE PERSON YOU KNOW YOU WERE CREATED TO BE!**

I can't do it for you. I can only write the books and present the material you need that will turn you in the right direction. I can mentor you, coach you, encourage you. But you, YOU have to do the hard stuff.

You have to dig deep to your very core and pull yourself up by the bootstraps to get to the place you want to be.

I am with you. My associates are with you. If you will help yourself, we can help you.

OK. It feels as though we have run a marathon, doesn't it? Only one more chapter and we will conclude. I hope you will read this book many times as you encounter what you have read throughout your life. This book is designed to help and encourage you through the very stressful seasons of life you go through. But, be encouraged because...

The Drill Sergeant says: YES, YOU CAN! YES, YOU WILL!

I am confident and have faith that you will make it and be **EXCELLENT!**

Drill Sergeant of Life-Tip #6 – F.O.C.U.S.

Get <u>F</u>ixed <u>O</u>n your <u>C</u>alling so you can experience <u>U</u>nusual <u>S</u>uccess

Action Steps

- Keep your mind focused on what YOU are doing. Put on your cosmic blinders and block out irrelevant material that causes you to question or doubt yourself.
- Be True To Your Calling. If someone attempts to sway you from your calling or purpose, step away from the person and S.T.E.P. into your purpose.
- Unusual Results come From Unusual Efforts. If you want something so extraordinary people everywhere will talk about it, you have to do something so extraordinary YOU talk about it first! Don't be ashamed of your calling! Give folks something to talk about.
- Successful People Think Success Thoughts. Your thoughts determine the level of success you ultimately achieve. If your thoughts are full of doubt, you will not achieve the results you desire. Line your thoughts and words up with the level of success you desire and you will have it!

Clarity Affirmation #6

I AM AWESOME AT WHAT I DO!

Conversely speaking, you are not awesome at what you don't do. So...

GET OVER YOURSELF, GET OUT OF YOUR OWN WAY, AND GET BUSY SO YOU CAN GET WHAT YOU WANT OUT OF LIFE!

Why is it we see ants during the spring, summer, and fall but never in the winter? Yet, they are back again and again, year after year? Because they work their little ant behinds off when they need to work their little ant behinds off! They work spring through fall so when the ground is mostly frozen and harvest is over, they survive from the work they have already done. Ants are awesome at what they do! Take a hint!

8 THE "UN" SIDE OF YOU

Wow! I applaud you! You made it through almost to the end. You are:

AWESOME!

MAGNIFICENT!

WONDERFUL!

You are all those things rolled up into one fabulous **YOU!** I am proud of you!

Many folks would have given up by now. How many people do you know who will allow a virtual stranger to get right in their face telling them, ***Get Over Yourself!*** *and* continue to read what the person has written?

How many folks do you know who will allow that same stranger to come in and attempt to change their way of thinking about themselves after they have been thinking this way for so long? Not many, I'll bet!

But, **you** are different. You want something different, something you can hold on to; something life changing! You want the dynamics in your life changed so you can make an impact in your world and in the people around you.

You are extraordinary!

You are ready to step away from *always* being the Bridesmaid or Groomsman and S.T.E.P. into your purpose of being the Bride or the Groom. Good for you!

You are ready for it! No one can take your purpose away from you. You were created for just this purpose for such a time as this.

Before we conclude, let's explore a side of you that you have never thought to explore: the "Un" side.

Now, by definition, the majority of words having the "un" prefix are mostly negative. But, do you know that you can always find positives in negativity? Let me show you.

After finally discovering your purpose and running like a mad-woman or man to fulfill it, the definition you once used for yourself and most people used for you now has to change. You have taken on a whole new persona!

- You are <u>unbending/uncompromising/unrelenting</u>. In other words, you stick to your own opinion, your own purpose and course of action in spite of myriad reasons others use for you **not** to pursue your purpose. You stick to your own opinion and purpose. You do not buckle under their arguments about failing because, they say, *you don't know what you are doing.* You choose to not be persuaded by their yammering.

  You have prayed about, meditated on, and **S.E.T.** your purpose in your mind and heart. Your brow is rock solid! You are not willing to be turned by anyone in spite of how much more they seem to know than you about your decision.

- You are <u>unfading/unflappable</u>. You are incapable of moving from or being moved by anyone else from your purpose. You pleasantly surprise yourself with your new attitude. You are pleased with your <u>unwillingness</u> to be swayed by those whose unsound advice you previously gave in to.

You are the trusty Rottweiler guarding the premises of his master. Loyally you stand ready to give your very life to keep out those who would invade. You guard your purpose with your life because it ***is*** your very life.

- You are <u>unyielding</u>. You are fully committed to achieving your goals; you will not slack off or yield. ***You are determination personified.*** You continue despite difficulties, opposition or discouragement. You persistently move toward excellence; you are more than capable of achieving what is set before you.

Your countenance is fierce as you consider what you have to do, are doing, and will continue to do as you pass milestone after milestone on your way to the fulfillment of your purpose. This is one time in your life when hardheaded and headstrong are good traits to display!

- You are <u>unshakable.</u> Although the road you travel is rife with adverse situations and circumstances, you neither panic nor get upset. You have not come this far to fail or die! You recognize those adverse situations and circumstances as merely hurdles you maneuver over and around on your way to the finish line of your destiny.

NOTE: Are you excited about your new season yet? I don't know about you but I am ready to burst! I am so excited for us!

- You are <u>untiring/unflagging</u>. You made a long, hard effort to get to where you are; this is only the beginning. Those who know you are amazed. You show no signs of weariness after working so hard. They see your efforts have tripled, quadrupled since you began. You are not letting up at all!

- You are <u>unashamed.</u> Gone are the moments of indecision, uncertainty, shame when asked what you are doing with your life. You stand toe-to-toe, boldly proclaiming your purpose. You dare the Naysayers and Unbelievers to show their silly heads. You are not ashamed to take up the Olympian torch of your cause: to boldly go forth by and with the power of Almighty God to do what you were created to do. You were born for such a time as this!

  As you go deeper into your purpose, Naysayers become "former" in nature. They unashamedly pat **you** on the back; they are so proud of you. Unbelievers convert: they believe with all their hearts that you walk in excellence in your purpose.

- You are <u>unconventional</u> in practice. Instead of conforming to your sphere of influence at large, you deviate from commonly accepted beliefs and practices.

***You no longer feel the need to do what
everyone else does.*** You no longer feel the desire
to get the same results they got. You want
something different! You are <u>unafraid</u> to blaze new
trails to your purpose, your destiny.

- You are <u>undivided</u> in thought. You learn to
F.O.C.U.S. You are not divided or scattered among
several areas of interest or concern. You are **F**ixed
On your **C**alling and experiencing **U**nusual
Success.

This new success is <u>unprecedented</u>; you have not
known or experienced this kind of success before.
You want to experience it even more. You desire to
be at the very top of your game.

- You are <u>unrivaled/unsurpassed.</u> You have no equal
or rival for excellence or desirability in your
purpose. You were created for this purpose; this
purpose was created for you.

- As you reach the top of your game, you find
<u>unspeakable</u> joy. You have never experienced this
before!

You are H.A.P.P.P.P.P.P.Y.Y. beyond measure;
and it shows. Your fountain of joy causes you to
overflow to others around you. **Everyone** wants
what you have. And you have only one piece of
advice for them:

GET OVER YOURSELF! *(Feels good to say it to someone else doesn't it?)*

- It feels good to have learned this important lesson for yourself. The result? You are <u>unlimited</u>, <u>unconquerable</u>, and <u>unstoppable.</u> You discover that the only limits to your life and purpose are the ones you impose upon yourself. No one else can limit you because **they** haven't given you the limitless potential you possess.

  As you flow deeper in your purpose, you realize you are incapable of being defeated, overcome, or subdued. Many giants dog your steps: giants of indecision, uncertainty, and fear to name a few. You put them in proper perspective and push yourself until you reach the next level in your journey.

  And what a journey it has been! You are <u>unstoppable</u>. You obtain clear passage without the usual obstructions. Excuses are a thing of the past. You continually break through strongholds that held you back. Those little voices of fear and doubt are quiet. They are replaced with the voices of faith and courage. *You are a changed person!*

No longer do you shiver at the thought of doing or learning something new. Instead, you run toward the new thing at full force. You know you are more than a conqueror. You can do all things because you have the strength, power, and wisdom of God the Creator within.

You can do all things through Christ Who gives you strength. And strengthen you He does! You can face it ALL!

...And the results?!? The new "Say-ers" (formerly Nay) shout for joy because, against all odds, you made it! In spite of opposition, you climbed out of mediocrity. You now sit atop Mount Excellence as the new Queen or King of the Hill!

Doesn't it feel wonderful? And the best is yet to come!

Although you have many miles to go, no one stops you. No one deters you. No one persuades you to leave the path you were commissioned to travel.

Through diligence, you acquire wisdom pertaining to your purpose through search and seizure. You search out wisdom for your given purpose and seize upon the ideas wisdom brings to you.

Not only do you acquire wisdom, you also obtain understanding. Wisdom and understanding travel hand-in-hand wherever they go. They team up with knowledge leading to a triple-fold blessing. With this tri-fold sword in your arsenal, you conquer any and everything!

So, how do you feel? (Honestly?) Apprehensive? Afraid? Angry? Doubtful?

Well, it's understandable. You have learned much about yourself during the time it took to read this book.

Mind you, none of this will come overnight. Because these ideas and concepts are foreign to you, you may need to read this material a second or third time before you finally get it. Don't give up!

Getting Over Yourself and Getting Out of Your Own Way may take some getting used to. After all, you didn't get here overnight.

It took years for you to become settled in the notion that you would *always* be a Bridesmaid and *never* a Bride; *always* a Groomsman, *never* a Groom. Once you accepted that knowledge, you went with it with no thought of changing that dynamic... Until now!

Quoth the Drill Sergeant, Never More!

You've come a long way, Soldier! It may take a little time, but you will overcome your Bridesmaid/Groomsman mentality!

Push yourself! Have faith and believe in yourself!

Your purpose is huge; it is stronger than you, larger than you. It can handle the emotions you experience.

Your purpose is patient. It has patiently waited all this time and will hang in there with you.

S.T.E.P. into your purpose. As you open yourself to your purpose, your purpose opens itself to you. As you make yourself available to your purpose, your purpose makes itself available to you.

Explore it, **search** it, and get it in your sights. Once you **target** it, **engage** it frequently so you can get the feel for it. Don't be afraid of your purpose. Very shortly, your purpose will prove to be the best friend you ever had.

Then, **proceed**. Come into agreement with it as you continue on the road of your journey. As you pick up other passengers – courage, endurance, persistence – you will find that you are having a grand old time with your purpose.

Come on!

GET OVER YOURSELF, GET OUT OF YOUR OWN WAY AND ENJOY THE RIDE AS YOU GET WHAT YOU WANT OUT OF LIFE!

Drill Sergeant of Life-Tip #7 – Reach For The Stars... Even If You Have To Tiptoe!

Action Steps

- Flow in your purpose. When you and your purpose move as one, you are unstoppable, unbeatable, and unapproachable.
- Discover your "Un" side. Adopt the 'un' words from this chapter into everyday life so you can become Unbelievable!
- Reach for the stars. There is a star for you. You don't have to catch hold of someone else's star: that star was made for that person, not for you. If you have to go into another constellation, stand on your tiptoes and do it! Your star is there for you; all you have to do is search and reach for it.

Clarity Affirmation #7

I AM UNSTOPPABLE!

The only obstacles able to stop me are the ones I place in front of myself. Nothing can stop me! I have clear passage to my destiny without obstructions.

9 THE CONCLUSION OF THE MATTER

The Drill Sergeant of Life says: *Get Over Yourself, Get Out Of Your Own Way, And Get What* YOU *Want Out Of Life!*

GET ON TOP OF THE WEDDING CAKE OF LIFE!

Now, understand: none of what I write or what you read means anything unless you take action steps to get to where you need to be. I can't force you to do anything.

Also, let's be clear on something: **You Are Awesome**! We all have some quirks, many faults, and numerous idiosyncrasies. None of these are insurmountable.

If we will but take the time to **Get Over Ourselves**, we will get on with our lives in amazing ways.

Now, one last time, let's go over our Drill Sergeant of Life-Tips and Clarity Affirmations. Get these things deep down inside of yourself. Use them continually.

Expect change to take place and it will. If you want change, **you** need to be the catalyst. Nothing will change if you don't.

So, let's begin with the Life-Tips and end with our Affirmations.

Drill Sergeant of Life-Tip #1 – Move From C.R.A.P.P.P.P.P.Y; make it S.N.A.P.P.P.Y so you can be H.A.P.P.P.P.P.Y.Y.!

- You are not here **to** hurt, degrade, gossip about, or persecute anyone. You are here to help, encourage, educate, and point Some Bodies in the right direction.
- You are not here **to be** hurt, degraded, gossiped about or persecuted by Some Body. Although we can't always control the actions of others in the way they treat us, we can always rise above their (and our own) expectations. We can take the High Road of Excellence instead of the Low Road of Bitterness and Mediocrity.

Drill Sergeant of Life-Tip #2 – S.T.E.P. into Your Purpose.

- **S.T.E.P. (Search, Target, Engage** and **Proceed)** into your purpose. You are here for a purpose. You were created for a particular purpose by God the Creator Who knows exactly what He is doing.
- Get over yourself and allow yourself to see things differently, to act differently, to do things differently. Your purpose will come forth with such clarity you will have no doubt what in the world you are here for.
- We are not here to **always** serve the purposes of others and **never** have our purposes realized. That's crazy! We all are here for Some Thing. We have to discover what Some Thing is for our lives. As we work with other people, helping them fulfill

their purposes, always keep in mind the fact that eventually, we will break off and do our own Thing.

- Get over the part of you that allows you to stay in the background and move forward into what you were created for.

Drill Sergeant of Life-Tip #3 – Dig Up and Destroy the Root of Your Excuses!

- You are one of the most awesome individuals ever created! (I am the other!) You are here to accomplish some of the greatest exploits of your lifetime. You were not created to be mediocre!
- Look at yourself! No; really **LOOK** at yourself! You are one of the most complex, highly intelligent, innovative people of your generation. The world rocks to your roll. You are a magnificent creature with more creative power in the tip of the pinky finger on your right hand than most people have in their entire Body! You have Donald Trump beat hands-down in money-making capabilities. You completely overshadow Sophia Loren with your beauty and charm. Your brain flows with such creative, analytical talent that Einstein, Curie, and Churchill *wish* they could return to this world so they could study at **YOUR** feet!
- **GET OVER YOURSELF AND STOP MAKING EXCUSES!** Excuses are a waste of your time! You have no time to waste in making your mark on the world!

Drill Sergeant of Life-Tip #4 – Have Faith and Believe in YOU!

- There is so much more for you to be, to do, and to have. The greatest minds of centuries past never had the brilliance displayed in their lives that shine around and through you constantly from the moment you arise in the morning until you go to bed at night!
- **Get over yourself, Get out there and Get your Stuff!**
- Don't sit back and wait for someone else to do what you are supposed to do! Make an impact on this world for your generation!
- Be more courageous than ever before. Do more of what you were called to do. Have more success than you have ever experienced!
- **Get Over Yourself and Do YOUR Thing!**

Drill Sergeant of Life-Tip #5 – Separate Yourself from Unbelievers

- Find your purpose and **S.E.T.** it in your brain. Write it down on flash cards. Take those flashcards with you wherever you go.
- Remember your purpose. Whatever you do, include your purpose. If you are able to work in your purpose every day, great! If not, make sure you incorporate some aspect of your purpose into everyday life so it is always before your eyes.
- Recite your purpose several times a day.
- Pray about your purpose. Meditate on your purpose continually.

- Be stubborn about your purpose without being obnoxious. If someone else tries to tell you what your purpose is, step back for a moment, remind yourself what your purpose is and politely but forcefully inform the person what your real purpose in life is.
- Don't take someone else's opinion about you as your own. Don't be afraid to change your scenery or atmosphere (that means ridding yourself of folks!)
- **Get Over Yourself and Stand Your Ground. Stay on Your Purpose!**

Drill Sergeant of Life-Tip #6 – F.O.C.U.S.

- Keep your mind <u>F</u>ixed <u>O</u>n your <u>C</u>alling and you will experience <u>U</u>nusual and <u>U</u>ndeniable <u>S</u>uccess.
- Wear cosmic blinders; never remove them. These blinders help you maintain your excellence focal point. They also prevent you putting your mind on things you have no business focusing on.
- Unusual efforts produce unusual results. If you multiply your efforts by 2, you achieve a result four times as much as expected. (**Your Effort x 2= Success⁴**)
- People around you are looking for something extraordinary to talk about. **GET OVER YOURSELF AND GIVE THEM SOMETHING TO TALK ABOUT!**

Drill Sergeant of Life-Tip #7 – Reach for the Stars even if you have to tiptoe!

- You are unstoppable! You are like the Atlantic and Pacific Oceans: you have boundaries but your boundaries are small considering your depth and parameters!
- When you flow in your purpose, you are simply amazing! Everyone sees your amazing single-mindedness and envy your focus and steel resolve.
- Reach for your own star, grab hold, and don't let go. That's your star! You were created for that star; that star was created for you. There are only billions of people in our universe; there are trillions of stars. Reach out and grab yours! If someone else is reaching for the same star, you can either let the other person have it or stand on your tiptoes!
- **GET OVER YOURSELF AND GO FOR IT!**

CLARITY AFFIRMATIONS

- I AM HERE <u>FOR</u> SOME BODY

- I AM HERE <u>FOR</u> SOME THING

- I AM HERE <u>TO DO</u> GREAT THINGS

- I AM HERE <u>TO BE, DO, AND HAVE</u> MORE

- I HAVE A S.E.T. PURPOSE

- I AM AWESOME AT WHAT I DO

- I AM UNSTOPPABLE!!!

This book was a pleasure to write! Truthfully, I learned much as I wrote each word, each Drill Sergeant of Life-Tip, each Clarity Affirmation.

I needed this book much more than you because I have lived each incident and example written here for 20 years. I finally broke free of the Always a Bridesmaid and Never a Bride Syndrome!

And now, I share these words with you. I hope and pray what you have read is beneficial, not only to you, but to each Body you touch and each Thing you create. I want to see you do the great things you were created to do. I pray that you be, do, and have more than you ever thought possible.

I believe in you. I have faith in your abilities. Now, you do the same for yourself!

God Bless and Keep You!

List of Acronyms and their Definitions

C.R.A.P.P.P.P.P.Y. – Can't Really Achieve your Potential because you (and those around you) continually Punish, Penalize, Persecute, or Put You(rself) down.

S.N.A.P.P.P.Y. – Start Now Achieving your Potential by Promoting and Pushing Yourself.

H.A.P.P.P.P.P.Y.Y. – Harvest Abundant Prosperity by being Passionate, Patient, Persistent and Purposefully Yielded to Your life.

S.T.E.P. – Search; Target; Engage; Proceed.

S.E.T. – Strategic; Evolving; Tactical.

F.O.C.U.S. – Fixed On Calling; Unusual Success.

ABOUT BEATRICE BRUNO, DRILL SERGEANT OF LIFE

Beatrice Bruno is a 15-year Active Duty Army Veteran but always and forever a Drill Sergeant! Having served in various assignments in the military, Beatrice admits that *"being a Drill Sergeant was the most rewarding two years of my life!"*

A Born-again Christian and ordained Gospel Minister, Beatrice has mentored and counseled people in all stages of life. Serving in ministry for the past 20 years, Beatrice has found that people from all walks of life have the same need: to **get over self and get out of their own way so they can get what they want out of life!**

Working from both sides of the spectrum, Drill Sergeant and Minister, Beatrice has developed a simple, no nonsense solution for getting out of the proverbial rut and moving forward in life to get what one desires to have in life: **Get Over Yourself, Get Out of Your Own Way, and Get What YOU Want Out of Life!**

8521934R0

Made in the USA
Charleston, SC
17 June 2011